BODY AND SOUL
A Study on the Christian View of Man

BODY
and
SOUL

A Study on the Christian View
of Man

by

D. R. G. OWEN

THE WESTMINSTER PRESS

Philadelphia

For Anne and Laura

Preface

IN AN EARLIER WORK (*Scientism, Man, and Religion*) I made the statement that most of the well-known conflicts between science and religion turn out, on investigation, to have been debates either between pseudo science and religion or between pseudo religion and science. In that book I attempted to define what I meant by pseudo science and to point out its mistakes. In the present work, I try to explain what I mean by pseudo religion and to expose its errors.

This attempt is made with special reference to the nature of man. In opposing the current naturalistic and materialistic estimates of human nature, it is all too easy to slip, by way of reaction, into some untenable form of body-soul dualism. I found myself repeatedly on the edge of this precipice in my attack on scientism. The questions were, therefore, raised in my mind: What exactly do we mean when we speak of " soul " or " spirit " in relation to man? And what exactly are the points of difference between the Christian and the naturalistic views of man?

This book is the result of my reflections on these questions. I hope that it will make some contribution to the discussion of the nature of man, a subject that is central in almost all the issues confronting us today.

D. R. G. OWEN

Contents

INTRODUCTION
Christianity and Scientific Naturalism

CHAPTER I

Christianity and
Scientific Naturalism

IN THE THIRTEENTH CENTURY, the imposing edifice of Christian thought, long in undisputed occupation of the field, was confronted with a serious challenge on the intellectual plane. The naturalistic philosophy of Aristotle was making a powerful reappearance in Western thought. Its Arabic exponents, Avicenna and Averroës, were enjoying a considerable vogue, especially in the academic circles of Paris and Oxford.[1] The orthodox Christian world-view found itself on the defensive, for the first time in centuries.

This revived Aristotelian naturalism, commonly known as Averroism, appeared at first sight to be an enemy of the Christian faith. It purported to explain the whole of reality by means of natural reason alone. The Christian view of things, based on revealed truth, was in danger of eclipse in the face of the growing influence of this kind of naturalism.

It was Saint Thomas Aquinas, of course, who met and overcame this challenge. By means of his synthesis of Christian truth and Aristotelian naturalism, he secured the survival and dominance of the Christian intellectual scheme for another two hundred years. And the significant fact is that Aquinas countered this naturalistic threat, not by repudiating, but by incorporating, its doctrines. Instead of anathematizing his opponent, he baptized him.

CHRISTIANITY AND MODERN SCIENCE

In the twentieth century, Christianity is again confronted by a serious challenge emanating from a naturalistic philosophy. This kind of naturalism, however, is not Aristotelian but scientific. It too attempts to explain everything by means of natural reason alone, but it defines natural reason in terms of the scientific method. Like the earlier version, it has won sweeping victories in intellectual circles, and in the face of its successes the Christian faith once again appears to be in danger of suffering intellectual defeat.

How is this challenge to be met? When faced with new and awkward questions, it is tempting, but in the long run unsatisfactory, simply to return to the answers that once before proved successful. It is necessary to meet the new questions on their own grounds. Here, as elsewhere in human life, " you can't go home again." A recovery of the *content* of Thomism, strongly advocated in some quarters, is not the solution of our present problem. Nevertheless, the *strategy and method* of Saint Thomas provide us with important clues.

The lesson that Aquinas has to teach us is this. We cannot afford to be indifferent or hostile to any of the knowledge that comes from sources other than the Christian revelation. It is fatal to adopt an ostrich policy and refuse to admit that natural knowledge has any bearing on Christian truth. The Christian faith is based on certain unshakable principles. But this does not mean either that we have yet fully grasped the meaning and implications of these truths or that the structure of Christian truth as a whole is static. Christian truth, like the Christian Church, is not a fixed and lifeless edifice, completed once and for all in the distant past, but rather a lively, growing organism. If it were a building that had been finished long ago, it would be subject to gradual deterioration and final collapse. It would eventually become obsolete and would have to be abandoned. But this is not the nature of Christian truth. Christ promised that his Spirit would *lead* us into all truth. And there is no reason to suppose that the guidance of the Holy Spirit, in this sphere, ceased to operate in the second, or the fifth, or the thirteenth, centuries. If modern science has enlarged the circumference of man's knowledge, we must regard it as the work of the Holy Spirit.

Natural knowledge (that is to say, knowledge acquired apart from special revelation) has always been highly esteemed, in the central Christian tradition, as part of God's general revelation. Knowledge of nature is especially important for a faith that believes that God, as the Creator, reveals himself in the whole natural order. A body of knowledge, therefore, such as modern science, that has discovered a vast array of new truths about nature has something of great importance to teach the Christian thinker. We neglect or oppose this knowledge at our peril. If the Christian faith is to survive, as a real power in the modern world, it must come to terms with modern science and with the modern philosophy of nature that is based on science. Taking our cue from Saint Thomas Aquinas, we must not repudiate but rather incorporate this scientific naturalism. We must not anathematize but rather baptize it.

The Thomistic synthesis, when it first appeared, was met with determined opposition from the reactionaries of the day.[2] Saint Thomas was attacked as a modernist and a liberal. A similar attempt at a modern synthesis will no doubt meet the same kind of obscurantist criticism. The self-appointed defenders of the " orthodox " and " Catholic " position will claim that science has nothing to teach us, that its theories are entirely irrelevant to Christian belief, and that the ancient dogmas of the faith achieved their final and unalterable form many centuries ago. The bigots, like the poor, we have always with us. And time has always proved them wrong. They have resisted every new advance in knowledge — the Copernican revolution in astronomy, the Darwinian hypothesis in biology, higher criticism in Biblical studies, the Freudian theories in psychology — and in every case they have eventually been forced to give ground in the face of overwhelming evidence.

Fortunately, there are many Christian theologians today who recognize the crucial importance of modern science and have made themselves at home in its various fields. We have only to recall the names of Karl Heim in modern physics, C. E. Raven in the biological sciences, Victor White and R. S. Lee in psycho-analysis, V. A. Demant and J. V. L. Casserley in the social sciences, and many others. We only wish it were possible to make a similar list of first-rate scientists who have made themselves familiar with Christian theology. For what is needed most of all is a cross-fertilization of minds on both sides, contributing, from many different angles, to the building up of a synthesis of Christianity and scientific naturalism. Because of the tremendous sweep of modern knowledge, such a synthesis could never be accomplished, as it was in the thirteenth century, by one man; it requires an army of scholars working in many different fields.

It will no doubt be widely admitted that what is needed today is a synthesis of science and religion. But why, it may be asked, do we refer not to science but to scientific naturalism, and not to religion but to the Christian faith? Taking the latter question first, it might well be suggested that the desired synthesis could more easily be achieved in the context of one of the other great world religions. Hinduism, for instance, is far more tolerant and syncretic than Christianity, and also has powerful Western advocates, such as Aldous Huxley and Gerald Heard. Or might it not be possible to establish a new religion, along the lines suggested by Julian Huxley, which could be broader, more humanistic, and better suited to modern knowledge?

In answering the question as to why we assume that the new synthesis must be made on the basis of the Christian faith, we point first of all to the highly significant fact, all too seldom recognized, that modern science was, in an important sense, the child of Christianity. It is obviously true, both that modern science took its rise in the *Western* world and that this world had been a *Christian* world for a very long time. Modern science began, not in a Hindu or Buddhist or Moslem or Confucian culture, but in a Christian culture. This initial conjunction of science and Christian civilization was not accidental; the latter was the necessary seedbed of the former.

A. N. Whitehead, who did not accept the Christian faith, has pointed out [3] that one of the fundamental assumptions of modern science is that the universe is rational. The whole purpose of science is to explain the universe in terms of rational order; it assumes that everything that happens is related to everything else in a rational, orderly system, and, according to Whitehead, science inherited this assumption from medieval Christendom. He attributes the highly developed medieval sense of order to three causes: first, the codification of Roman law and its application throughout the Holy Roman Empire, resulting in a strong sense of legal order; [4] second, the widespread "habit of definite exact thought," [5] emanating from scholastic philosophy; and finally, most important of all, the Christian idea of God. "The inexpungible belief that every detailed occurrence can be correlated with its antecedents in a perfectly definite manner, exemplifying general principles," had its origin in

"the medieval insistence on the rationality of God, conceived as with the personal energy of Jehovah and with the rationality of a Greek philosopher. Every detail was supervised and ordered: the search into nature could only result in the vindication of the faith in rationality." [6]

We might venture the generalization that the content of a theology (an idea of God) always has important consequences for the content of a cosmology (an idea of nature). With this in mind, there are good reasons for claiming that the view of nature on which modern science is based could have arisen only against the background of the Christian idea of God. Other theologies entail quite different cosmologies. As Whitehead says:

" In Asia, the conceptions of God were of a being who was either too arbitrary or too impersonal for such ideas to have any definite effect on instinctive habits of mind. Any definite occurrence might be due to the fiat of an irrational despot, or might issue from some impersonal, inscrutable origin of things. There was not the same confidence as in the intelligible rationality of a personal being. I am not arguing that the European trust in the scrutability of nature was logically justified even by its own theology. My own point is to understand how it arose. *My explanation is that the faith in the possibility of science, generated antecedently to the development of modern scientific theory, is an unconscious derivative from medieval theology.*" [7]

If this is the case, another question at once arises: Why did modern science take its rise, not in the high Middle Ages, but only when medieval Christendom was disintegrating? Doubtless there are many reasons. One of them has been emphasized by Michael Foster,[8] followed by John Baillie.[9] The medieval Christian philosophers were inclined to interpret the rationality of the universe in Greek rather than in Biblical terms. The main stream of Greek philosophy tended to suppose that the universe flows from God as a geometrical theorem flows from the definitions and axioms. If this were the case, then the rational order of the universe could be logically deduced from the nature of God, and there would be no need for any reference to empirical observation. Thus, medieval " science," following the Greek pattern, was mainly deductive in method. First, discover the first principles of all things, and then deduce the logical consequences; observation, sense-experience and experiment are of relatively little importance. Modern science, on the other hand, while it has its deductive aspects, is highly inductive in method; it proceeds from observation of particular facts; one cannot deduce the nature of things by pure thought but must proceed slowly by careful and prolonged observation. The nature of things is rational, but its rationality is not a logical necessity. The order of nature is a rational order, but what this actual order is has to be worked out by patient empirical investigation.

"What is the source," asks Foster,[10] "of these un-Greek elements in the modern science of nature by which the peculiar characteristics of the modern science of nature were to be determined?" Both Foster and Baillie answer that the source is again Christian, this time the Christian doctrine of creation. It is true, as Whitehead said, that the rational, deductive element in modern science comes from the medieval idea of the rationality of God, but Whitehead failed to develop the implications of his own reference to "the personal energy of Jehovah."[11] For Greek thought, God *had* to make the world as it is. Its features are the logical consequences of his nature; it could not be other than it is. The Biblical doctrine, however, is not that the world proceeds necessarily from the divine Reason but that it is a creation of the divine Will; it might have been other than it is. This does not mean that the creation was a purely arbitrary act. For, in the Biblical view, the divine Will acts in accordance with the divine Wisdom or Logos. But

"we must not say that there were no alternatives between which the divine Wisdom had to choose. From that it follows that while everything in nature observes a rational pattern and is therefore in principle intelligible by us, we cannot know in advance which rational pattern it is going to follow."[12]

This is exactly the assumption on which modern science is based: the order of nature is rational, but has to be worked out by careful empirical investigation, and cannot be logically deduced. This assumption could not be derived from the Greek theology, with its exclusive emphasis on the divine Reason, or from the Moslem theology, with its one-sided stress on the divine Will, any more than from the Hindu theology. It could stem only from the Christian idea of God, which recognizes both divine Reason and the divine Will.

Moreover, it is not only that the Christian conception of God led to that special *view* of nature that made possible the modern scientific *knowledge* of nature. It is also true that the Christian theology entailed a conception of man's *relation* to nature that prepared the way for the modern scientific technological *control* over nature. In the Biblical story of creation, God says of men, " Let them have dominion over . . . all the earth " (Gen. 1:26). As long as man was more or less completely immersed in nature, as long as he lived in dread of the demons that were supposed to inhabit nature, as long as he embraced an animistic view of nature (such as we still find in Greek thought and other higher religions), so long it was impossible for him to detach himself sufficiently from nature, and to take a sufficiently objective view of it, to control and master it. It was the Biblical teaching about man's proper relation to nature that destroyed the demons and put an end to animism and nature worship. Only then could science begin to subdue nature by building its vast technological structure. As Berdyaev said, " For man to be able to treat nature like a mechanism, it is necessary for the demonic inspiration of nature and man's communion with it to have died out in the human consciousness." [13] It was Christianity that brought about the new attitude to nature, and for this reason it is proper to say " that Christianity alone made possible both positive science and technics." [14]

Exactly the same point may be made in connection with man's relation to society. The New Testament teaches that the only society to which man belongs by absolute right is the Kingdom of God. Judged by the criterion of the Kingdom, all the societies that have ever existed fall short, and none of them can claim man's unquestioning allegiance. As long as man was entirely dependent on the existing social tradition, as long as he worshiped totems and other symbols of the apotheosis of the social structure, he could never rise above it sufficiently to shape and control it in accordance with his own deliberate choice. Just as Christianity released man from bondage to nature, so it emancipated man from servitude to society and put an end to totem worship.[15] This was also necessary as a preliminary clearing of the ground, only accomplished in a Christian culture. It was then that science was able to begin its investigations into social organization and to launch out upon that program of " social engineering " by which the social structure, like the forces of nature, is to a considerable extent brought under man's conscious control.

These are the facts to which we point when we say that modern science, at its inception, was based on assumptions about the order of nature and about man's relation both to nature and to society that were Christian in origin. It was for reasons such as these that modern science arose in a Christian and not in a Hindu, Buddhist, Moslem, or Confucian culture. It would seem, then, reasonable to suggest that a philosophy based on science could be reconciled to Christianity more readily than to any other religion.

CHRISTIANITY AND NATURALISM

We have been speaking of a possible synthesis between *scientific naturalism* and the Christian faith, instead of between *science* and religion. The reason for this is that the body of knowledge we call science does not belong to the same level of thought or realm of discourse as the Christian faith. The Christian faith consists of beliefs that make up a general world-view. Science is a collection of particular theories about particular aspects of the world. There is, however, a world-view that is based on science; it is this that we refer to as scientific naturalism. It belongs to the same level of discourse as the Christian intellectual scheme and can be compared with it. No doubt it is this scientific naturalism that is usually the referent of the word " science " in the phrase " science and religion." If we use it in this sense, as we shall for the sake of convenience, we shall write it " science " and not science.

The only one of the great world religions about which it is even possible to raise the question of a synthesis with this scientific naturalism is Christianity. For not only is science a child of a Christian culture, but it is also perfectly proper, as we shall see,

to speak of Christian naturalism — whereas, of course, it would
be absurd to speak of Hindu or Buddhist naturalism. Indeed, the
main difficulty in the way of any reconciliation between " science "
and " religion " is that " science " is preoccupied with nature,
matter, and this world, while religion is supposed to be entirely
concerned with the supernatural, the spiritual, and the next world.

Now while this may be true of religion in general, it amounts
to little short of a caricature of the Christian faith. We recall
William Temple's famous saying that Christianity is " the most
avowedly materialist " of all the great religions.[16] He was drawing
attention to the same features of Christianity to which Albert
Schweitzer refers in his distinction between the Christian faith as
" world-affirming " and the religions of India as " world-denying."
Oriental religion in general tends to treat the whole realm of
nature as *maya,* as illusion, as a sphere of unreality from which
the human soul must by all means escape; it is antiphysical and
antinatural. Christianity, on the contrary, teaches that the whole
natural, physical order is God's creation and, as such, is both real
and good. It is not something from which man is destined one day
to escape, but something that he is meant to control and use, and
his relationship to it has eternal significance. And it is not only
the Christian doctrine of creation but also the Christian doctrines
of the incarnation, the resurrection of the body, and Christ's return to the earth at the end, that make us take the physical order
seriously, recognizing that it has an eternal place in God's purposes.[17]

It is this Christian naturalism in the realm of doctrine that lies
behind the Christian concern for this world in practice. It is in
the Western world, therefore, with its Christian background, and
not in the East, where other religions have prevailed, that we find
the beginnings of various humanitarian movements and a general
preoccupation with man's material well-being, unknown in
cultures built on different religious foundations.

This Christian naturalism, both in theory and in practice, indicates that it is with Christianity and not with any other religion that scientific naturalism can be reconciled. The other religions are preoccupied with the supernatural and "the things of the spirit"; they are so uniformly world-denying and world-escaping that these features are almost the defining characteristics of "religion" as such. It is for this reason that we have refrained from speaking of the Christian "religion." For Christianity is not a religion in this sense at all. Yet this is the sense in which the word is usually used in the phrase, "science and religion." As in the case of "science," so in the case of "religion," when we use the word in this sense, we shall write it "religion" and not religion. And there can be no synthesis between "science" and "religion," for they stand in direct opposition to one another. The most that could be hoped for would be a division of labor in which the things that belong to nature and to this world are altogether surrendered to "science," while "religion" continues to restrict itself to the things that belong to the spirit and to the next world. Fortunately, however, we are not driven to this desperate solution as far as Christianity is concerned, for Christianity is not a "religion."

If Christianity is thus naturalistic and materialistic, our former question recurs in a slightly different form. Why did the concern for man's material welfare and for the things of this world have to wait, like the appearance of science, for the beginning of the modern period of Western history when the Christian Middle Ages had come to an end and the Christian faith was becoming a waning influence? The answer again is that medieval Christianity was influenced not only by Biblical naturalism but also by Greek metaphysical dualism. The influence of Greek thought created a Christian version of "religion" in which the natural and the supernatural were ranked in a two-story structure, with the main honors going to the supernatural to the disparagement of the earthly and the natural. Medieval Christianity to this extent corrupted the Biblical world-view and turned men's minds away

from this world to the "higher" heavenly places. Christianity
thus tended to become a "religion" like other "religions."

In this connection scientific naturalism, by recalling us from
Greek and Oriental otherworldliness to a proper and Biblical
concern with this world, can render a great service to genuine
Christianity. The scientific naturalism that has become characteristic of modern Western thought has, in George McLeod's words,
"brought man down to earth." From the Christian point of view,
this is sheer gain, since it sheds new, or forgotten, light on the
old Biblical proclamation that *God* has come down to earth. It
cannot be right for the Christian, who believes in this earthward
movement of God, to oppose or disparage this modern earthward
movement of man. As C. S. Lewis says, "There is no good trying
to be more spiritual than God." [18] We must recognize that this
naturalistic development in the Western world has taken place
within, and not outside, the purposes of God. In George Mc-
Leod's words:

"Gerald Heard may write with some truth that 'Newton banished
God from nature, Darwin banished him from life, and Freud drove
him from his last stronghold: the soul.' But is that to finish the matter? Man's honesty in pursuit of truth — whatever the first apparent
results of such pursuit — cannot really be a flight from God. Surely
it is more sensible to suppose that God had a mighty purpose in bringing man 'down to earth.' Whatever chaos man's pride has created
along the roadside of this journey, we believe that this journey was
also of God. Just as Christendom [medieval culture] was necessary
to the fashioning of one stage of man's journey, so also, in the purpose
of God, this 'earthing' of man has been necessary." [19]

The naturalism of a scientific age can help to purify the Christian
faith of its "religious" accretions. Genuine Christianity is not
"spiritual" and otherworldly; it is naturalistic and this-worldly.
There is, therefore, no irreconcilable opposition between the Christian and the "scientific" world-view.

It is not only Christianity, however, that tends to be corrupted.
Scientific naturalism, on its side, very often deteriorates into

" scientism." [20] Preoccupation with nature can easily lead to the dogma that nature is a closed and self-explanatory system, that matter as we know it is the ultimate reality, and that explanation in terms of natural cause and effect gives the final truth. This kind of crude materialism carries with it a denial of the reality of spirit and freedom in any sense. And science is invariably invoked to support these conclusions. Such dogmas distort science into " science " or " scientism," just as the Greek and Oriental doctrines, on the other side, pervert Christianity into " religion." And just as " religion " can lead to otherworldliness and escapism, in which the values of this life tend to be dismissed as worthless, so " science " can easily result in some kind of " scientific " mass society, in which the true values of human existence tend to be destroyed.

If there is to be a reconciliation between scientific naturalism and the Christian faith, then both sides must begin by mending their own fences. The genuine truths of scientific naturalism, based on scientific evidence, have to be carefully distinguished from the illegitimate conclusions of " scientism." On the other side, Christians must distinguish just as clearly between the authentic truths of the Christian faith, based on Biblical sources, and the alien accretions of " religion." It is to this latter task that the present work is mainly devoted.

THE NATURE OF MAN

In attempting to make a contribution to the reconciliation of Christianity and modern naturalism, we are confining ourselves to a preliminary clearing of the ground. But our contribution is still more circumscribed. For we shall restrict ourselves to one part of the vast field. Our main intention is to elucidate the real nature of the Biblical-Christian view of man. This is, therefore, an essay in Christian anthropology. We shall use the word " anthropology " here, not in the usual contemporary sense in which it stands for one of the social sciences, but in its broader etymological meaning, where it stands for a general theory or doctrine of man.

It is in the field of anthropology, in this general sense, that the conflict between "science" and "religion" is sharpest at the present time. In fact, the two views of man are hopelessly antithetical. The irreconcilable nature of this opposition would not be a matter of any great concern were it not for the fact that it is regularly mistaken for a conflict between the actual scientific evidence and the genuine Christian estimate of human nature.

We hope to expose this mistake by showing that the "religious" anthropology is not Christian but Greek and Eastern both in origin and in nature,[21] and that it is this view of man, and not the Christian, that the scientific evidence refutes.[22] In the course of the argument the authentic Christian doctrine will be elicited,[23] and it will then be obvious that this view is perfectly consistent with the evidence collected by the various sciences. At the same time, we shall have to distinguish between the scientific evidence proper and the "scientific" materialism to which the evidence, in some quarters, is supposed to lead.[24]

The points at issue revolve around the concepts of "body" and "soul." The "religious" anthropology adopts an extreme dualism, asserting that the body and the soul are two different and distinct substances. It claims that the soul is divine in origin and immortal by nature and that the corruptible body is the source of all sin and wickedness. It recommends the cultivation of the soul in detachment from the body, and advocates the suppression of all physical appetites and natural impulses. It regards the body as the tomb or prison of the soul from which it longs to get free. Finally, it tends to suppose that the soul, even in its earth-bound existence, is entirely independent of the body and so enjoys a freedom of choice and action untrammeled by the laws that reign in the physical realm.

The scientific evidence, on the contrary, indicates that "body" and "soul" are simply the names of two inseparable aspects of a unified psychosomatic whole. It follows, therefore, that there can be no detachable part of man that survives physical death. The sciences of man have also taught us that the rigorous suppression of natural instincts and desires can do incalculable injury to the human personality. The same investigations have further revealed the extent to which the beliefs, conduct, and character of the individual are shaped by material forces operating in accordance with general laws. In other words, the evidence appears to refute the fundamental doctrines of the " religious " anthropology.

The faults, however, are not all on one side. The " scientific " anthropology supposes that the same evidence that refutes the " religious " view leads inevitably to a crudely materialistic interpretation of man, to a free self-expression ethics, and to some form of absolute determinism. Against these extreme doctrines we can see that the " religious " anthropology, in spite of its mistakes, stands for and protects certain important truths about man's status, especially the reality of the human spirit and of human freedom.

Nevertheless, our main concern must be to set our own house in order. If scientific naturalism tends to deteriorate into scientism, the Christian faith seems even more prone to degenerate into " religion." And nowhere does this happen more often or with more disastrous results than in the field of Christian anthropology.

We are frequently surprised and shocked by the theological illiteracy and naïve misunderstandings of Christian beliefs that turn up repeatedly in otherwise well-informed writers, especially on popular scientific subjects. In commenting on Fred Hoyle's *The Nature of the Universe*, Professor J. V. Langmead Casserley cites a typical example:

" The problem of whether or not it is possible for man to transcend and conquer death he confuses with the question whether a part of man, called his ' mind,' has within it some inherent property which gives it the power to survive the dissolution of the body. He doubts whether it has, and so, I venture to think, would any competent Chris-

tian theologian. The Christian belief is certainly a belief in the full
mortality of man — and, equally certainly, not a belief that some one
part of human nature is inherently immortal." [25]

Casserley is right in his statement of the genuine Christian position in this matter. Unfortunately, however, his historical generalization about Christian theologians is more questionable. The
fact is that many Christian teachers and preachers have undoubtedly presented, as Christian, precisely the view that Hoyle is opposing. He probably learned it at Sunday school, and, in the unlikely event of his attending church, he would certainly hear it
preached in any one of a great many pulpits on almost any Sunday. The point is that we cannot lightly dismiss, as culpable
ignorance, the misinterpretations of Christian doctrine that are
so common on the part of its opponents. Erroneous teaching, on
the part of Christians themselves, must bear a large share of the
blame.

It is not only in preaching and teaching that we encounter
traces of the " religious " anthropology. It turns up, even more
often and more objectionably, in many so-called Christian hymns,
prayers, and poems. The opening sentence of the body of com-
mittal in the Burial Office of *The Book of Common Prayer* is
starkly dualistic: "Forasmuch as it hath pleased Almighty God
of His great mercy to take unto Himself the soul of our dear
brother here departed, we therefore commit his body to the
ground." [26] A phrase in another prayer in the same Office betrays
not only dualism but also a Greeklike, " spiritual " contempt for
physical existence: "With whom the souls of the faithful, after
they are delivered from the burden of the flesh, are in joy and
felicity." The Orphic notion that the body is the tomb from which
the soul longs to get free is clearly set forth in the lines of the
Christian poet, John Donne: " When bodies to their graves, souls
from their graves remove." [27]

Many of our hymns are nothing but thinly disguised Orphic
poems. How frequently we are asked to lament this present life

as a " weary pilgrimage " and " transient dream," and to hate the physical aspects of our being as shackles binding us to earth, and to look for an eventual release and an escape to heaven, " up above the sky."

> " Here in the body pent,
>   Absent from Him I roam,
>   Yet nightly pitch my moving tent
>   A day's march nearer home."

Examples in allegedly Christian hymns of " religious " escapism, hostility to this life, and otherworldliness could be multiplied indefinitely. It is beyond question that the " religious " view of human life frequently turns up disguised in Christian clothes.

If we turn to the Bible, however, as we shall later,[28] we find that a quite different view of man is assumed throughout. Here there is no dualism and scarcely any idea of the immortality of a detached and independent soul. There is no tendency to ascribe unrestricted freedom of choice to the soul, nor is there the slightest inclination to vilify the body and its appetites. On the contrary, the Bible assumes that human nature is a unity; in the New Testament it teaches that man's ultimate destiny involves the " resurrection of the body," that in actual fact the human will is not free but in " bondage," and that a repressive and legalistic system of ethics is an intolerable burden that authority " binds " upon men's shoulders.

One of the most important contributions that Christians can make to the eventual reconciliation of Christianity and scientific naturalism is to rid their thinking of the spurious intrusions of " religion." It is an essential prolegomenon to the main task.

PART ONE

The "Religious" View of Man

CHAPTER II

The Origin
of the "Religious" View

WE CAN DEFINE the "religious" anthropology as the view of man that makes a sharp distinction between the body and the soul, regarding the latter as pure, holy, and immortal, and the former as evil, earthy, and corruptible. Human existence is here thought of as a miserable and unfortunate episode in the life of the soul, whose true home is elsewhere. The escape of the soul from the body and from the defilement of matter in general is to be accomplished by a rigorous suppression of the physical appetites and passions.

It is commonly held that this "religious" anthropology originated in the Western world in the last three centuries before Christ during the Hellenistic period and was imposed in strength on Western culture by early Christianity. Classical Greek culture is said to have maintained a quite different view of human life and to have assumed for the most part a naturalistic, well-rounded interpretation of human nature and human happiness. Professor Mary White represents the typical position of classical scholarship when she writes of Greek civilization that "it did not set up any conflict between body and soul, appetites and reason. The spiritual agony of reconciling such a conflict, and of freeing the soul from the corruption of the body was a later development.[1] " This she assigns to the third century B.C., and she goes on to say:

"The *sōma-sēma* formula was one expression of it, the body as the prison house for the soul; another form was the doctrine that the soul must be purged of the corruption of the body before it can attain the

vision of truth or enjoy complete happiness. This antithesis between
the flesh and the spirit is found in the New Testament in many passages: it is more frequent than the other view of the body as 'the
temple of the Holy Ghost.' As in so many other fields, the contact
between classical and Christian thought came when the older classical
view had itself actually suffered serious modification. The result was
many centuries of mortification of the flesh before the balance was re-
stored." [2]

Leaving on one side, for the present,[3] the complete misunderstanding of the New Testament contrast between the "flesh"
and the "spirit," we should notice how the impression is here
conveyed that the "religious" view of man appeared late in
Greek thought and became prevalent only under the influence
of Christian theology. Now, in actual fact, all the ideas mentioned
in this passage are found in Greek thought at least as early as the
sixth century B.C., and are widespread in the classical literature of
the fifth and fourth centuries. Professor White, of course, is aware
of this fact; she would argue, however, that this view of man is
not typical of classical Greek thought and represents only a minor
strain that is out of harmony with the prevailing ideas. Our main
point is that this "religious" anthropology is Greek and not
Christian in origin, that it turns up too often in the classical
period to be set aside as a weak and unimportant element in
Greek life, and that where it occurs in the early Christian writings
it is a Greek intrusion and not a development of the Biblical
point of view. We must now turn to the evidence.

EARLY GREEK THOUGHT

Where the ideas in question appear in Greek literature they are
usually labeled "Orphic." Whether or not there was a well-defined
religious cult called "Orphism" is a disputed question. But the
point that concerns us here is that there are numerous references
in fifth century writers like Herodotus, Empedocles, and Ion of
Chios that establish the fact that, whether or not these ideas should
all be grouped together as "Orphic," they are certainly taught as

early as the sixth century B.C., and are prevalent in the fifth.

We should not expect to find in the sixth century any philosophical or psychological analysis of human nature. What we find are myths and ritual practices which clearly imply a certain view of man's origin and destiny. And, of course, the etiological and eschatological ideas of a philosophy or a religion always afford important clues for the understanding of its anthropology.

The " Orphic " myth of man's origin is assigned by Pausanias to the sixth century B.C.[4] This is sometimes questioned, but the story is archaic in character and seems to have been known in full by Plato at the end of the fifth century.[5] The myth tells how the Titans, who were offspring of Heaven and Earth, slew Dionysus, the son of Zeus, and ate his flesh. Zeus thereupon consumed them with a thunderbolt, and out of their remains there sprang the race of men. Thus man was born of the most wicked sons of Earth. The original, Titanic sin haunts him all his days. This sin is associated with his earthy, physical parts which are by nature corrupt and bad. At the same time man possesses a divine and heavenly part. For the Titans were sons of Heaven as well as of Earth, and the fragments of the divine Dionysus, which the Titans devoured, went into the making of man. Thus man is a dual creature, and his most strenuous efforts must be directed at purging away the earthy, titanic element so that the divine and heavenly part can return to its true home with the gods. This appears to be the significance of the " Orphic " purificatory rites and the Dionysian ritual which aimed at escape from the body and union with the god in its ecstatic climax. The same implications are suggested by some inscriptions found in tombs in southern Italy and Crete; they are fifth century and appear to be taken from a presumably well-known " Orphic " poem: " I am a child of Earth and starry Heaven but my race is of Heaven "; " I have flown out of the sorrowful, weary circle, I have reached my goal "; " Thou hast become god from man, happy and blessed one." [6]

These words lead us on to the " Orphic " myth of man's final destiny. This is the familiar story of the soul's transmigration, re-counted by Plato in several of his dialogues:[7] souls existed at first in the highest heavens, but some fell and were forced into bodies; they are condemned to successive reincarnations for a period of ten thousand years; at the end of this time, if they have sufficiently purified themselves, they will return to their heavenly home.

A quite definite anthropology is clearly suggested by these myths. Man consists of two independent substances, a soul and a body. The soul comes from, and by nature belongs to, a higher, heavenly realm. It is therefore never at home in this world but passes through it as an unwilling alien. Physical existence is a punishment and a calamity; the bodily appetites and pleasures are bad and must be suppressed. The limitations were carried out in practice not only in purificatory rites but also, apparently, in mildly ascetic rules, like vegetarianism.[8]

According to Plato and Philolaus, the " Orphics " made their anthropology even more explicit in the theory that the body is the prison of the soul — the famous *sōma-sēma* doctrine. In the *Cratylus,* Plato discusses the derivation of the word *sōma;* he suggests that it comes from *sōzesthai,* meaning " to keep safe " or " to shut up " as in prison: " In my opinion," he writes, " it is the followers of Orpheus who are chiefly responsible for giving it the name, holding that the soul is undergoing punishment and has this husk around it like a prison." [9] In another dialogue he says " I have heard from some wise men that in our present state we are dead and the body is our tomb." [10] Philolaus states that " the ancient theologians and seers bear witness that for purposes of punishment the soul is yoked together with the body and buried in it as in a tomb." [11]

This sixth century Greek view, then, holds that man's earthly existence is a living death in which the soul has become trapped in a body. It teaches that the soul must be purified of its bodily contaminations in order to escape from earthly limitations and defilements and return to the heavenly realm of pure spirits. In view of this evidence alone we should have to reject Professor White's unqualified statements that the Greeks " did not set up any conflict between body and soul, appetites and reason," and that " the spiritual agony . . . of freeing the soul from the corruption of the body was a later development." One school of Greek thought certainly did " set up a conflict between body and soul " and this development was by no means " late "; it began at least as early as the sixth century which inaugurated the great age of Greece.

GREEK PHILOSOPHY

Numerous fifth century references [12] make it clear that the set of ideas that we have called " Orphic " was adopted by Pythagoreanism. This was an important and influential school of religion and philosophy founded by another somewhat shadowy sixth century figure. The association of " Orphism " and Pythagoreanism is so close that Ion of Chios [13] can suggest that Pythagoras wrote poems under the name of Orpheus, while Herodotus, in speaking of " things called Orphic," says they are " really Egyptian and *Pythagorean*." [14] As a religious order, the Pythagoreans adopted body-soul dualism, transmigration with its corollary of the heavenly origin and destiny of the soul, and those ascetic and purificatory practices which imply hostility to the physical appetites. Philosophically, the Pythagoreans rationalized the " Orphic " myths, with important consequences for later Greek thought, especially Platonism. They taught that there were three ways in which the soul could be purified of its bodily contacts — the ascetic, the aesthetic, and the intellectual. Of these, the intellectual way, in which the soul is subjected to rational form, was the highest and best. Thus the soul began to be associated with pure reason; its true end lay in escape from the body and in return to the higher heavenly realm which was similarly defined in terms of pure, mathematical rationality.

Of other sixth century Greek philosophers, it is possible that Anaximander and Heraclitus were influenced by " Orphic " teaching. In the oldest extant fragment of Greek philosophy, Anaximander seems to be saying that this world is essentially a place of punishment and expiation.[15] And according to a late and, admittedly, unreliable source, Heraclitus said that " when we are alive the soul is dead and buried in us, and when we die the soul comes to life again." [16] We are on much stronger ground, however, when we come to the fifth century philosopher Empedocles, for his religious poem, the *Katharmoi* is highly " Orphic " in tone.[17]

The " Orphic " influence on Greek thought is strongest and most important in the greatest of all Greek philosophers, Plato, who lived from 427(?) to 347 B.C. As we have already seen, he takes over many of the " Orphic " myths of the soul. His philosophy is, to a considerable extent, a rationalization of these myths in which their philosophical implications are drawn. His proofs of the immortality of the soul are mainly concerned to show its kinship with ultimate reality, the realm of pure and eternal rationality; the soul always has existed and always will exist. The doctrine of reminiscence, another important element in his philosophy which explains the possibility of human knowledge, also presupposes the divinity and eternity of the soul.

This theory of the nature of the soul involves, of course, a radical dualism. The soul belongs to the higher, divine and rational, realm, the body to the lower and mortal sphere. This body-soul dualism is clearly stated by Plato in many passages. In one place he says that " the soul is in the very likeness of the divine and immortal and intellectual and uniform and indissoluble and unchangeable; the body is in the very likeness of the human and mortal and unintellectual and multiform and dissoluble and changeable." [18] In another place he speaks of " the composite of body and soul we call man." [19]

The soul is defined in such passages as pure reason. Its aim is to escape from the body and from this world. The body and the

world are not only hindrances and limitations but also the source
of all evil and corruption. The body and its desires must therefore
be suppressed as enemies of the soul. Thus we find, as we shall
again and again, that the radical separation of soul and body is
accompanied by hatred and contempt for the body. This hostility
to the body is given the strongest possible expression by Plato:

> " The true philosopher will despise [the pleasures of the body]
> . . . he is entirely concerned with the soul and not with the body.
> He would like, as far as he can, to get away from the body . . . to
> dissever the soul from the communion of the body . . . Thought is
> best when the mind is gathered into herself . . . when she takes
> leave of the body and has as little as possible to do with it . . . And
> in this the philosopher dishonors the body . . . While we are in the
> body and while the soul is *infected with the evils of the body,* our
> desire for truth will not be satisfied. For the body is the source of
> endless troubles . . . diseases . . . lusts . . . fears, fancies . . . fight-
> ings, factions . . . It has been proved to us by experience that if we
> would have pure knowledge of anything we must be quit of the
> body . . . and then we shall attain the wisdom we desire . . . not
> while we live but after death . . . In this present life I reckon that
> we make the nearest approach to knowledge when we have the least
> possible intercourse with the body . . . We keep ourselves *pure* until
> the hour when God himself is pleased to *release us.* And thus having
> got rid of the foolishness of the body, we shall be *pure* and hold con-
> verse with the *pure.*" [20]

A little later, in the same dialogue, Plato makes Socrates say:

> " I go on my way rejoicing, and not only I but every other man who
> believes that his mind has been made ready and that he is in a manner
> *purified* . . . And what is *purification* but the *separation of the soul
> from the body,* the *release of the soul from the chains of the body* . . .?
> The true philosophers are always preoccupied in the practice of dying
> . . . If they have been in every way *enemies of the body,* wanting to
> be alone with the soul [they will welcome death] . . . [True philos-
> ophers] *despise the body.*"

This last passage brings us to Plato's conception of the ultimate
destiny of the soul. The purified soul will in the end return to

the divine and heavenly realm from which it came. Losing its individuality, along with its body, it will be absorbed into pure, universal reason. The way to achieve this end is the purification of the soul through intellectual endeavor and the philosophical pursuit of knowledge:

" The soul which is *pure* at departing and draws after her no *bodily taint,* having never voluntarily during life had connection with the body which she is ever avoiding, herself gathered into herself, and, making such withdrawal her perpetual study . . . departs to the invisible world, to the divine and immortal and rational." [21]

From these passages it is clear that for Plato the true status of the soul is that of disembodied existence in the realm of pure reason which is both its origin and its destiny. The body is something quite alien to the soul and bodily existence is a sheer calamity. It would be difficult to find a more unambiguous assertion of body-soul dualism with its antiphysical corollaries. And this is *Plato* speaking, the voice of classical Greek culture.

It is true that in the *Republic,* Plato modifies the extreme dualism of the earlier dialogues. He recognizes that the physical desires, being conscious states, must be included in the soul, even if only as the lowest part. But at the end of this work, where he recurs to his favorite theme of the immortality of the soul, we find that it is still the rational part only that is destined for immortality; reason will eventually escape even from the lower parts of the soul and will return to the sphere of pure reason:

" We were thinking just now of the soul as composed of a number of parts . . . , and such a composite thing could hardly be everlasting . . . That the soul is immortal is established beyond doubt . . . but to understand her real nature we must look at her, not as we see her now, *marred by association with the body* and other evils, but when she has regained that *pure condition* which the eye of reason can discern . . . We must fix our eyes on her love of wisdom (the activity of the rational part) and how she seeks to apprehend and hold converse with the divine, immortal, and everlasting world *to which she is akin,* and what she would become if her affections were entirely set on following this impulse . . . *disencumbered* of all that wild profusion of rock and shell whose earthy substance has encrusted her because she seeks what men call happiness by making earth her food." [22]

In the *Timaeus,* written after the *Republic,* Plato is still sounding the same tune: he speaks of reason as "the lordly part of the soul . . . which raises us up from earth toward *our kindred in heaven.*" He goes on:

"He who has seriously devoted himself to learning and to true thoughts . . . must necessarily and inevitably think thoughts that are immortal and divine and partakes of immortality in so far as it is possible for human nature . . . making that part [of the soul] that thinks like unto the object of its thought in accordance with its original nature, and having this likeness attain finally to that goal of life which is set before men." [23]

Reason is man's true soul; it is this alone that is divine and immortal and that will ultimately escape from the limitations and corruptions of the body into the real of pure, universal reason. Plato remains to the end an antiphysical dualist. It is he, and his followers, who most of all are responsible for imposing the "religious" anthropology on Western thought.

Plato's great student, Aristotle, the only other claimant to the role of Greece's greatest philosopher, made a determined attempt to interpret man in other than dualistic terms. He sharply criticized Plato's dualism (which he called "*chōrismos,*" or "separation"), both in reality in general and in man in particular. For Aristotle, reality is not to be divided into two radically different realms. The ultimate unit is the concrete individual substance. Each substance, to be sure, has two aspects: first, its universal, rational aspect or form, which it shares with all other members of the same class, and, second, its particular, physical aspect or matter, which makes it an individual thing. Thus a table shares the same general pattern (its form) with all other tables of the same kind, while the physical stuff of the table (its matter) makes it this particular table and not another table. The various kinds of substances that constitute nature are ranked in a hierarchy in accordance with the degree to which their form achieves complexity and dominates their matter. At the bottom of the scale are inorganic substances, where the form is simply physical organization. Next come vegetable substances, in which the faculties of reproduction and nutrition are added to organization. At a higher stage are the animals, which possess consciousness and desire. Finally, at the highest level of nature, there is man, who is distinguished from everything else by the faculty of reason. At all but the lowest level we can speak of form and matter as soul and body. This does not now, however, imply any dualism, since soul and body are no longer thought of as two different substances but merely as two aspects (the form and matter) of the same one substance.

At this point Aristotle appears to have overcome the old body-soul dualism. Man does not consist of two distinct and radically different parts. He is, rather, a unified substance in which soul and body are not two different kinds of thing but simply the form and matter of the same single substance. And since the substance is the ultimate reality, and since every substance necessarily consists of both form and matter, we expect Aristotle to go on to say that neither can exist apart from the other. But it is just at this point that Aristotle is unable to resist the pressure of the tradition of thought to which he belongs; he returns to dualism.

Nature, with its substances made up of form and matter, does not exhaust reality, on Aristotle's view. Above and beyond nature is Pure Form, Form unmixed with matter. And this Pure Form is once again Pure Reason, which is divine and eternal. Thus Aristotle ends with a metaphysical dualism which is not so remote, after all, from Plato's. Similarly, in his anthropology, it turns out that reason in man is a spark of Pure Reason, a divine element in man's nature. It can raise man completely above nature and, when cultivated by the pursuit of knowledge, can finally escape altogether from matter and become united with the divine, Pure Reason.

So Aristotle also arrives in the end at a version of the familiar "religious" anthropology. The fact that he did so, in spite of himself and in spite of his opposition to the Platonic "separation," is evidence of the strength that the dualistic tradition had by this time achieved in Greek culture.

Just how influential in Greek life generally was this set of ideas known as "Orphism" or the "religious" anthropology? The fact that these ideas were undoubtedly advocated, in a quite extreme form, by three of the foremost Greek philosophers, namely Pythagoras, Empedoclês, and Plato, together with the possibility that they influenced early Greek thinkers like Anaximander and Heraclitus, is not entirely without bearing on the question as to the extent to which they permeated Greek culture in general. Philosophy is not written in a vacuum; the picture of the philosopher in his ivory tower is overdrawn. The fact is that the philosophy of a period is very often simply the rational articulation of the typical assumptions of the time. Even on the basis of this evidence alone, the evidence drawn from Greek philosophy, it is impossible to regard these "Orphic" ideas as a minor trend, a weak and obscure element in the Greek attitude to life.

There is, however, a not inconsiderable amount of evidence from other sources. For example, these same "Orphic" ideas were familiar to and were utilized in various ways by the great fifth century poets and dramatists.[24] They were used by Pindar in his second Olympian Ode. They turn up in a fragment of Euripides' *Cretans,* and were apparently prominent in a lost play by Aeschylus called the *Bassarids.* Cicero is the not very trustworthy authority for the statement that Aeschylus was himself actually a Pythagorean. Aristophanes, of course, wrote a parody of an Orphic poem in *The Birds.* Finally, there are the inscriptions, previously referred to, written on thin gold plates which have been found in tombs in southern Italy and Crete and identified as belonging to the fifth century; they are evidently quotations from an "Orphic" poem, and they served the same purpose, and presumably were as popular, as the lines that are frequently inscribed nowadays, on tombstones.

If we put together all this evidence from Greek philosophy, literature, and epigraphy, it seems apparent that the "religious" anthropology was of early origin in Greek culture and was widespread throughout the fifth and fourth centuries. Its main doctrines were body-soul dualism, exaltation of the soul and the immaterial in general as divine and eternal, denigration of this life and this world, and suspicion of the physical appetites. In view of the evidence cited here, the view that classical Greek culture "did not set up any conflict between body and soul" and that "the spiritual agony . . . of freeing the soul from the corruption of the body was a later development" would seem to require some qualification.

The other part of the thesis, that is almost the stock in trade of classicists and humanists, is that the New Testament and the Early Church were responsible for implanting the "religious" anthropology in Western civilization. As far as the Bible is concerned, we shall argue later on [25] that the Biblical view of man is in fact radically different and that there is in the Bible little trace of the "religious" ideas in their Greek form. With reference to the teaching of the Early Church, we shall go on to show in the next chapter how the extreme versions of the "religious" anthropology, so popular in the Hellenistic world, were labeled immediately as heresies by the Church authorities and were, at certain points, relentlessly attacked by the Church Fathers. At other points, it is true that certain elements of these pagan philosophies crept into the thinking of the early Christian apologists. But where this happened it can be shown that alien elements have been superimposed on Biblical ideas. The Biblical ideas are in themselves essentially different and remain in uneasy alliance with the Greek partners that are forced upon them.

EASTERN RELIGIONS

Before proceeding with this line of thought, it may be instructive to pause for a moment to notice that very much the same " religious " view as that which entered the Western world from Greece was also current in the East, beginning at the same time or earlier. In fact, since this kind of anthropology forms a part of so many different religions, it seems appropriate to call it " religious." The interpretation of human life in terms of dualism, with its antiphysical bias and its idea of the immortality of the detached and separate soul, seems to be typically " religious."

There is a sense (but not the popularly accepted sense) in which it is true to say that all religions teach the same thing. The development of religion seems to be fairly uniform everywhere up to a certain point. We find, for instance, more or less the same manifestations appearing at the primitive stage of religion in widely scattered parts of the world. Belief in spirits, mana, fetish, taboo, totem, sacrifice, and magic appears universally at this level. After the primitive stage we find another common development in the direction of animism, polytheism, and crude supernaturalism. We may cite here the Olympian religion of Greece, the Vedic hymns of India, the religions of Babylonia and Egypt, of Persia before Zoroaster, and of Arabia before Mohammed. The third stage of development, also common to most religions, is represented by the set of ideas that we have called the " religious " anthropology or " Orphism." It is only after this stage has been reached that there is more or less sharp differentiation into the great world religions, Hinduism, Buddhism, Judaism, Christianity, and Islam.

Among the few exceptions to this general law of religious development were the Hebrews, who appear never to have experienced the " Orphic " stage to any appreciable extent. Consequently, the New Testament, with its Hebrew background, shows little trace of " Orphic " beliefs. Nevertheless, because " Orphism " is " religious " in the general sense, Christianity, in the course of

its development, is constantly tempted to embrace some of the
tenets of the "religious" anthropology. We shall see how this
happens when we come to examine the history of Christian
thought on this subject.[26]

In India the ideas in question appear so early and are so prevalent that it has been suggested that "Orphism" actually derived its inspiration from that quarter. It is probably closer to the
truth to hold that these doctrines are characteristically "religious"
and turn up spontaneously in different places. However that may
be, it is certainly the case that Hinduism and, to a lesser extent
Buddhism, fully adopted this view and never went beyond it in
their doctrine of man. We find it, for instance, in familiar form in
the Upanishads, which became part of the sacred Hindu scrip-
tures between the eighth and fifth centuries B.C. This version dif-
fers from the Greek only in substituting spirit for reason as the
highest and purest kind of being both in man and in reality in
general. In its cosmic aspect it is known as Brahman; as the soul
of the individual it is called Atman. The soul of man is still regarded as a spark of the divine which, somehow or other, has
become trapped in a body. Still the soul must pass from one body
to another through a weary cycle until at last it is purified and
can return to the Absolute from which it came.

We have here, then, a set of ideas very similar to the Greek:
the same radical dualism between spirit and matter, the same
exaltation of pure spirit, the same doctrine of transmigration, and
the same denigration of this world. In fact, this tendency is exaggerated in the Upanishads to the point where matter is not only
despised as inferior and bad but dismissed as unreal and illusory.

The doctrine of salvation in Hinduism is also similar to the
way of escape in the Greek view. The soul or Atman must be
purified of its contaminations with the body by means of, first,
ascetic practices: suppression of all appetites, self-tortures, concen-
tration, and self-hypnotism induced by Yoga and other similar
systems; and, second, intellectual effort leading to all knowledge,

especially knowledge of the identity of Atman and Brahman.
This will eventually result in complete escape from the body,
from individuality, and from the whole material realm, and in
the attainment of absolute oneness with Brahman.

In the following passage from the Upanishads, it is not difficult
to discover the familiar doctrines of dualism, the divinity of the
soul, transmigration, hostility to the body, and the expectation
of future disembodied blessedness in union with the Absolute:

" He, the highest Person [Atman], who is awake in us when we
sleep . . . that indeed is Brahman, that alone is called immortal . . .
If a man does not understand this before the falling asunder of his
body, then he has to take body again in the world of creation . . .
[But] having understood that the senses are distinct [from Atman]
and that their rising and falling belongs to them in their distinct
existence, a wise man grieves no more . . . Every creature that knows
Him [Brahman] is liberated and obtains immortality . . . This, the
firm holding back of the senses, is what is called Yoga . . . When all
the ties of the heart are severed here on earth, then the mortal becomes
immortal . . . Let a man draw that self [Atman] forth from the body
with steadiness, as one draws the pith from a reed . . . Having received this knowledge, taught by Death and the whole role of Yoga,
Nakiketas became free from passion and death and obtained Brahman." [27]

The same " Orphic " tones continue to be sounded in later parts
of the Hindu scripture. A typical passage from the Bhagavad-Gita,
probably dating from the second century B.C., speaks of the soul
or Atman as

" eternal, indestructible, and indefinable . . . it is not born nor does
it ever die nor, having existed, does it exist no more. Unborn, everlasting, unchangeable, and primeval, it is not killed when the body is
killed . . . It is everlasting, all-pervading, stable, firm, and eternal."

The same section goes on to give expression to the familiar antiphysical bias:

" For the enjoyments born of contact between senses and their objects are, indeed, sources of misery . . . A wise man feels no pleasure

in them . . . To the ascetics, who are free from desire . . . the Brahmanic bliss is on both sides of death. The sage, who excludes from his mind external objects . . . who restrains senses, mind, and understanding, whose highest goal is final emancipation . . . is, indeed, ever released from birth and death . . . Abandoning, without exception, all desires . . . and restraining the whole group of senses on all sides by the mind only, one should by slow steps become quiescent . . . and fixing one's mind upon the self [Atman], should think of nothing." [28]

Gautama Buddha, the great religious genius of India who belongs to the sixth century B.C., was brought up as a Hindu and continued to share the Hindu estimate of matter in general as bad and ultimately unreal. He also remained faithful to the doctrine of transmigration and the hope of a future state of disembodied blessedness. In other respects, however, he rejected the ancient religion of India and founded his own. He seems to have been completely agnostic about Brahman, and he certainly denied the reality of the soul in man. He cannot, therefore, be accused of dualism. In place of the soul, he postulated desire as the force that holds together the component parts of the individual, survives death, and reconstitutes the components in successive incarnations. The goal of life is nirvana, which is achieved by the extinction of desire in every form, especially physical desires.

This was the teaching of Gautama himself. However, his agnosticism and denial of the soul were too " irreligious " for his followers, most of whom relapsed into polytheism and " Orphism." The more philosophical writings of historical Buddhism are scarcely distinguishable from the Greek and Hindu thought of the kind we have noted. The following example is taken from the *Surangama Sutra* of the first century A.D.:

" Ananda, can you not see the difference in nature in that which moves and changes and that which is motionless and unchanging? It is the body that moves and changes, not mind . . . As one forgets the true nature of mind, so he mistakes the reflections of objects as being his own mind, thus binding him to the endless movements and changes and suffering of the recurring cycles of deaths and rebirths that are of his own causing. You should regard all that changes as ' dust particles ' and that which is unchanging as being your own true nature of mind. . . .

" [Then they] besought the Lord Tathagata to teach them to make distinctions between mind and body, between real and unreal, between the manifested natures of death and rebirths, on the one hand, and the intrinsic nature of that which is unborn and never dies, on the other hand, the one appearing and disappearing, the other forever abiding within the essence of their own mind." [29]

There can be little doubt that the ideas of the " religious " anthropology were common in both India and Greece as early as the sixth century B.C. From that time on they have unquestionably exerted an important influence on the whole of human life in India. The quietistic and world-denying emphasis, as long as it continued, resulted in indifference to the things of this world, in acquiescence in the social *status quo,* and in failure to make any kind of progress in the improvement of man's earthly lot.

Under the inspiration of Christianity, the history of Western civilization has been very different. In spite of the black marks on its record, it cannot be denied that Western civilization has added enormously to man's material well-being. This could never have happened in the West, any more than in the East, if the Christian faith had been as " Orphic " in its view of human life as were the religions of the East. Classicists and humanists to the contrary notwithstanding, in the history of Western culture " Orphism " is a Greek and not a genuinely Christian product. In the patristic and medieval periods, Christianity was sometimes in danger of being corrupted by these Greek ideas. But fortunately this danger was, for the most part, overcome, partly because of the sanity and durability of the authentic Biblical teaching and partly because of the vitality of modern science; the this-worldly emphasis and the true naturalism of the Biblical faith have triumphed over the world-denying spiritualism of " religion."

CHAPTER III

The "Religious" View
in Early and Medieval
Christian Thought

WE SHALL NOW PROCEED to examine the influence of the "religious" anthropology on Christian thought from the second century A.D. down to the end of the Middle Ages. We shall find that the typical doctrine of man expounded in this period is a mixture, purporting to be a synthesis, of Biblical and Greek categories. This type of amalgamation is, of course, characteristic of Christian philosophy and theology generally in the patristic and medieval periods. It has been said that Christian philosophy filled the forms of Greek thought with the substance of the Biblical revelation. In many cases the old bottles proved inadequate to contain the new wine and occasionally burst apart under pressure.

THE PAGAN PHILOSOPHIES

The early Christian philosophers and theologians, commonly known as the Church Fathers, were writing in the period from the second to the fifth centuries A.D. They were trying to explain, defend, and propagate the Christian faith in a largely Greek-thinking world. The forms and categories, as well as the language, of current thought were Greek in character. And this characteristic way of thinking about life and reality was not only Greek but was an exaggeration of all the tendencies that we have previously examined. In this Hellenistic world, there was, in the first place, an extreme metaphysical dualism, dividing reality into two completely separate and distinct realms: a higher, rational and divine realm, which was alone fully real, and a lower, irrational and material realm, which was regarded either as incompletely real or as altogether illusory. Secondly, in line with this kind of metaphysics, there was a corresponding anthropological dualism, dividing man into two more or less unrelated parts: the soul, belonging to the divine realm and therefore by nature pure and immortal, and the body, belonging to the material sphere and so mortal and impure. Finally, stemming from these doctrines, there was a radical antiphysical bias that regarded the physical, both in reality and in man, not only as inferior and corruptible but also as intrinsically evil. All these ideas were deeply entrenched in the world into which Christianity came and to which the Church Fathers were attempting to communicate their faith. The " religious " anthropology was taken to the most exaggerated lengths in Gnosticism, Neoplatonism, and Manichaeism, the typical pagan philosophies of the Western world in the second and third centuries A.D.

The early Christian apologists, like apologists in every age, had to speak the language of their hearers. They had to speak Greek, both literally and metaphorically. They had to learn, not only the words, but also the categories and thought-forms of their intellectual contemporaries. In other words, they had to translate the great Biblical concepts into Greek terms. There was no other way in which they could successfully preach the gospel in their day. In fact, of course, this process antedates the Church Fathers. The Old Testament had long before been translated into Greek in the Septuagint, and the New Testament books were written in the Greek language. To what extent Greek *ideas,* as well as Greek *words,* were already present in the later books of the Old Testament and in the New Testament is a question we must reserve for later treatment.[1] But it is clear that the Fathers, in order to speak to their age, had of necessity to steep themselves in the Greek way of thinking and the Greek way of looking at things. It was inevitable, therefore, that they should absorb almost unconsciously some of the elements of the Greek view of life. We shall not be surprised, then, to find some traces of the "religious" anthropology in the writings of the Church Fathers.

THE CHURCH FATHERS

The first point to emphasize, especially in relation to the familiar canard that Christianity was responsible for propagating spirit-matter dualism and the corresponding disparagement of all things physical, is that these ideas, as current in the pagan philosophies of the time, were immediately labeled as *heresies* by the Church. Gnosticism, Neoplatonism, and Manichaeism were the objects of constant and strenuous attack by the Christian apologists. What is remarkable about the Church Fathers is, not that they absorbed some of the ideas of their time, but that they were so largely successful in resisting the great pressure of the climate of opinion in which they lived.

As soon as this has been said, it has to be admitted that writers like Clement of Alexandria, Origen, and others, who have been described significantly as "the Christian Platonists of Alexandria,"[2] were very close to being Gnostics themselves. And, of course, it is well-known that Saint Augustine, the most influential of all the apologists of this period, was by turns a Manichaean and a Neoplatonist before his conversion. Nevertheless, it remains true that even the most Hellenistic of the Church Fathers stood out from their non-Christian contemporaries in an extraordinary way, and not least in their anthropology. What distinguished them especially was their refusal to share in the current intellectual denigration of the body and of the physical in general. This refusal, as we shall see, was dictated by allegiance to the Old Testament doctrine of the creation of the physical universe by God and the New Testament insistence on the resurrection of the body.

We may say that the Church Fathers generally adopted a "high" view of the body in contrast to the antiphysical bias of the contemporary pagan philosophies. This "high" view of the body is stated by many of the early apologists. In the second century, Justin Martyr sharply criticized the Hellenistic philosophers because "they abuse the flesh, adducing its infirmities, and declare that it only is the cause of our sins." [3] His grounds for rejecting this position are the doctrines of creation and the resurrection of the body:

"It is evident, therefore [from Scripture], that man made in the image of God was flesh. Is it not then absurd to say that the flesh made by God in his own image is contemptible and worth nothing? But that the flesh is with God a precious possession is manifest first from its being formed by him." [4]

Concerning the doctrine of the resurrection of the body, he wrote:

"Is it not absurd that that which has been produced . . . and which is *beyond all else valuable* should be so neglected by its Maker as to *pass to nonentity* . . ., that God would so neglect his own possession and work that it becomes *annihilated and no longer exists* . . .? But in truth he has even called the flesh to resurrection, and *promises to it everlasting life.*" [5]

The body is part of the image of God in man. It is created by him and is destined, not for "nonentity" or "annihilation," but rather for "everlasting life." It is therefore "precious" and "beyond all else valuable" and is not to be neglected or despised. This is as far as may be from the typically "Orphic" contempt of the body. The orthodox Christian apologists of the Early Church cannot justly be blamed for the spread of this latter attitude. On the contrary, they opposed it as vigorously as possible.

Irenaeus, in the same century, also appealed to these two Biblical beliefs as the grounds for a "high" view of the body. But he went even farther and argued, on the basis of the Biblical revelation, that the whole physical order has a place in God's ultimate purposes; the physical universe is not destined either " to pass to nonentity ":

> " ' But I say unto you, I will not drink henceforth of the fruit of this vine until that day when I will drink it new with you in my Father's kingdom.' He promised to drink of the fruit of the vine with his disciples, thus indicating two points: the *inheritance of the earth* in which the new fruit of the vine is drunk, and the resurrection of his disciples in the flesh . . . And he cannot by any means be understood as drinking of the fruit of the vine when settled down with his own above in some supercelestial place." [6] (See Appendix.)

These Christian apologists expected no future state of disembodied blessedness in the immaterial heavens. This aspect of the " religious " anthropology was also repudiated; God's purposes for man would be consummated here on earth. In all this, Justin and Irenaeus were simply remaining faithful to the Biblical teaching in opposition to the " Orphic " assumptions of their age.

In the third century, the Latin Father Tertullian went so far as to claim that the soul was corporeal. What precisely he meant by this is by no means clear since he also insisted that the soul, in contrast to the body, was spiritual and immortal. But in defending his view of the corporeality of the soul he used many arguments that are similar to those used to support the modern notion that man is a psychophysical unity,[7] especially the argument from the numerous examples of reciprocal influence between the body and the soul.[8]

Gregory of Nyssa, in the next century, continued this line of thought. He recognized, in a strikingly modern way, both the thoroughgoing interaction of mind and body and also the physiological basis of sensation and thought. These facts are fatal to radical body-mind dualism. Gregory pointed out that thought cannot function at all apart from the physiological nervous system and the physical brain.[9] He showed how the relationship between the mind and the body is so intimate that the proper function of the former depends on the health of the latter, so that

if the latter is in any way impaired, "the movement of the intellect halts correspondingly." [10] He concluded from these facts that
in man "the union of the mental with the bodily presents a connection unspeakable and inconceivable." [11]

In accordance with this "high" view of the body, regularly
adopted by the orthodox exponents of Christianity in the first
four centuries, the Church Fathers also uniformly refused to identify the body as the source of sin. Justin Martyr strongly opposed
those who thought of the soul as pure, and associated sin with the
physical appetites. "In what instance," he asked, "can the flesh
possibly sin by itself, if it have not the soul going before it and
inciting it?" [12] Clement of Alexandria, who was closer than most
of the Fathers to Gnosticism, adopted the authentic Christian
position on this point: he insisted that it is the will and not the
body that is the source of evil in human life.[13] Similarly, Tertullian defined the essence of sin as willful disobedience to divine
law.[14]

Gregory of Nyssa, in dealing with the same question, referred
as usual to the interrelation of body and soul:

"Our soul has touch with . . . and is knit up with . . . all those
phenomena in us which we call the ' passions,' which have not been
allotted to human nature for any bad purpose at all (for the Creator
would most certainly be the author of evil if in them, so deeply
rooted as they are in our nature, any necessities of wrongdoing were
found) but according to the use which our free will puts them to,
these emotions of the soul become the instruments of virtue or of
vice." [15]

A few pages later, he exposes the self-contradiction inherent in
the Gnostic position: the Gnostics say that the soul belongs to a
pure and heavenly region from which it fell by reason of sin and
is imprisoned in the body as a punishment; at the same time,
they condemn the body as the source of evil, failing to notice
that this is inconsistent with their view that sin is *prenatal*.[16]

Finally, Saint Augustine, who had once been a Manichaean,

severely criticized the philosophy he had formerly embraced precisely on the grounds that it associated evil with matter. Both in the *Confessions* [17] and in the *City of God* [18] he stated emphatically that sin is due, not to the body, but to the misuse of free will. In the latter work, in the passage cited, he interpreted Saint Paul's use of the phrase " the flesh " as meaning, not the body, but the whole man in his sinful condition; [19] human vices do not proceed from the body alone but from a misdirection and corruption of the whole personality: " the corruption of the body is not the cause but the punishment of sin." [20]

In all this it is obvious that we have a view of the body and a definition of sin that are entirely different from the " Orphic " and Platonic doctrines. As long as the Fathers are faithful to the Bible, they cannot be accused of setting up " a conflict between body and soul, appetites and reason." The body was made by God and was therefore good. It was not to be despised or vilified.

At the same time we find in some of the Fathers, especially in the " Christian Platonists " and in those on the fringe of orthodoxy, a certain suspicion of and hostility to the physical passions. This is, no doubt, to be explained partly as a necessary reaction and opposition to the licentiousness and sensuality of the society in which they lived. But some of them certainly went far beyond the proper demands of moderation and self-control. They slipped away from the Biblical position and into the " religious " anthropology. Thus, for instance, Tatian, a second century writer who is rightly regarded as partly heretical, is said to have condemned marriage as " defilement and fornication," [21] and to have pronounced " all sexual intercourse as impure." [22] We find the same tendencies in Clement of Alexandria in his view that Christ's human nature must have been exempt from all carnal desires, even the most necessary and innocent, [23] and in his suggestion that the sin of Adam and Eve may have been that they anticipated the time set for their marriage by God. [24] An extreme case of antisexual puritanism is Origen's notorious act of self-castration. It is not surprising that in Origen's philosophy the physical appetites are very nearly condemned as in themselves evil. But Origen, like Tatian, was, significantly enough, suspected of heresy at several points.

It has to be admitted, however, that there were antiphysical strains in writers as highly orthodox and influential as Gregory of Nyssa and Saint Augustine. The former, in spite of his knowledge of body-soul interaction, wrote some very Platonic passages in which he deprecated the physical desires as such:

> " Those that are still living in the flesh must, as much as ever they can, separate and free themselves in a way from its attachment by virtuous conduct, in order that after death they may not need a second death to *cleanse* them from the remnants that are owing to *this cement of the flesh,* and when once *the bonds are loosed* from round the soul, her *soaring up* to God may be swift and unimpeded, with no *anguish of the body* to distract her . . . When the change is made into the impalpable unseen, not even then will it be possible for the lovers of the flesh to avoid dragging away with them . . . some *fleshly foulness.*" [25]

The " Orphic " notes in this passage are very different from the attitude to the body-soul relationship that Gregory elsewhere expressed. The truth is that he wavered between a materialism that was suggested by his knowledge of physiology and was also closer to the Biblical position, and a false spiritualism that was derived from his knowledge and love of Greek philosophy.

Something of the same kind appears in Saint Augustine. In spite of his Biblical understanding of the nature of sin, he seems to have had a special horror of vices associated with the physical appetites. Again this may be partly explained as a reaction to the excesses of the secular society with which he was familiar as well as to the overindulgence of his own pre-Christian life. In any case, he came close at times to Tatian's condemnation of sexual intercourse, even in marriage. In one passage he described marriage as " the reputable enjoyment of voluptuousness." [26] In the famous passage in which he described his conversion, he pictured himself as struggling against his physical passions: "Why not now, even at this very hour, is there not an end put to my uncleanness? Thereupon I heard the voice of a boy or girl singing, '*Tolle lege, tolle lege.*'"[27] He took up the Bible and it fell open at Rom. 13:13: "Not in rioting and drunkenness, not in chambering and wantonness, not in strife and envying: but put ye on the Lord Jesus and make not provision for the flesh to fulfil the lusts thereof." It is plain enough how he is here interpreting "the flesh," and it is significant that this particular verse, so understood, should have been the immediate occasion of his conversion.

We see in these tendencies of some of the Fathers both the beginnings of that exaggerated and fanatical asceticism that was later to characterize the so-called Christian solitaries and anchorites, and also the seeds of an antisexual bias that was at least a factor in the development of clerical celibacy.

Nevertheless, in the orthodox eschatology of the Fathers a "high" view of the body was once again asserted in the strongest possible terms. They all accepted the Biblical assurance of the resurrection of the body, and this, along with the doctrines of creation and incarnation, made it quite impossible for them to succumb to the Gnostic, Neoplatonic, and Manichaean contempt for the earthy in general. The body, as well as the soul, belongs to the essence of man. And if the soul survives the body, as most of the Fathers believed, its existence in that state is incomplete; it must wait upon the recovery of its body at the last day before it can enjoy the fullness of personal being. "For what is man," asked Justin Martyr,

"but the reasonable animal composed of body and soul? Is the soul by itself man? No; but the soul of *man*. Would the body be called man? No; but it is called the body of *man*. If then neither of these is by itself man, but that which is made up of the two together is called man, and God has called *man* to life and resurrection, he has called not a part but the whole, which is the soul and body."[28]

This is the typical teaching of the Fathers. Moreover, they regularly argued that the resurrection body is the same body as the present one, though glorified and transfigured. " The resurrection is the resurrection of the flesh that died," said Justin.[29] Similarly, as we read earlier in Irenaeus, the whole earthly realm, marvelously transformed, will be the locale of God's consummated purpose, the site of the City of God. (See Appendix.)

As we have seen, this " high " view of the body was sometimes accompanied by a certain suspicion of the physical appetites. Nor did it appear to be incompatible with a strong belief in the immortality of the soul. This latter belief especially — the idea that the soul can exist apart from the body — obviously implies some form of body-soul dualism. This is clear already in the passage just quoted from Justin Martyr in which the body and the soul are specifically called different " parts " of man.

This body-soul dualism was a necessary implicate of the Greek doctrine of the immortality of the soul. The Fathers thought it necessary to incorporate this latter belief into their teaching, and were therefore almost bound to adopt some kind of dualism as well. Now there are a few isolated Scriptural passages that may suggest the idea of the immortality of the soul in the Greek sense, but the normal Biblical point of view is quite different: in the New Testament it is the resurrection of the body that is stressed, and this doctrine is almost a direct contradiction of the " Orphic " eschatology. Why, then, did the Fathers lean toward this largely un-Biblical notion? The answer may be, in part at least, as follows: The New Testament writers, because of their expectation of the imminent end of all things, never really faced the question: What happens to the individual between the time of his death and the time of the general resurrection at the last day? For them, the end was expected at any moment. But as time went on, the end was more and more deferred, and so this question became increasingly pressing. To the Fathers, the answer was all too readily available in the form of the prevalent Greek doctrine: the soul

as an independent substance is immortal and survives the death
of the body. If this is so, then it follows that the soul is different
in kind from the body, and we arrive, inevitably, at dualism.

The " religious " anthropology, however, was modified by the
Fathers at this point in two ways. In the first place, the " religious " view held that the disembodied existence of the soul
was its ultimate destiny. This could not be accepted by the Fathers
because of their allegiance to the Biblical teaching of the resurrection of the body. They therefore attempted to combine the
" religious " and the Biblical doctrines. The disembodied soul,
they said, awaits the recovery of its body in the consummation
of all things at the end. The existence of the soul apart from the
body is, therefore, an intermediate state. In the second place, the
" religious " view taught that the soul was *by nature* immortal,
and therefore not only always *would* exist but always *had* existed.
This doctrine of the pre-existence of souls was almost unani-
mously rejected by the Fathers, once again because of their faith-
fulness to the Biblical position. Souls, like everything else, are
created by God, and therefore could not have existed eternally.

The next question that arose was whether souls, once they had
been created, were then by nature immortal and imperishable.
Here there was a difference of opinion. Justin Martyr argued [30]
that the soul was not necessarily immortal because, like all created things, it was liable to corruption. Most of the Fathers, however, believed that God created souls in such a way that they could
not die. The favorite arguments that they employed to prove this
contention were the three familiar Platonic " proofs." First, some
activities of the soul, notably rational thought, are completely
independent of the body; therefore, the soul is independent of
the body and of bodily death. Secondly, the soul is the very principle of life and, therefore, cannot know death, which is the opposite of life. And, thirdly, death is the dissolution of the elements
of a composite substance; but the soul is a simple substance and,
therefore, cannot be dissolved.

These three arguments turn up repeatedly in the patristic writings.[31] And they clearly commit the Fathers to some form of body-soul dualism. This comes out most strongly in Saint Augustine, who, in arguing for the immortality of the soul along the usual Platonic lines, does not hesitate to define man as " a rational soul using a mortal and earthly body." [32] He also states unambiguously that the soul is a substance in its own right and with a nature of its own.[33]

The fact is that the Fathers' adoption of the " religious " idea of the immortality of the detachable soul forced them into the doctrine of body-soul dualism. This doctrine was modified, however, by their continued allegiance to the New Testament teaching of the resurrection of the body. The result of this attempt to hold together two quite different views was the doctrine of the intermediate state. After the death of the body, the soul survives in a different mode of existence and waits to be reunited with its body at the last day.

The idea of the intermediate state eventually developed into the doctrine of purgatory. This development began as early as Justin Martyr. He said " the souls of the pious remain in a better place, while those of the unjust and wicked are in a worse, waiting for the time of judgment." [34] A similar idea is found in Irenaeus.[35] Gregory of Nyssa significantly called the intermediate state by the Greek name " Hades." [36] He also appears to have been the first to assign to it a specifically purgatorial function. It is the scene of " healing " or " curing " of souls by fire. Some are cleansed from evil in this life, others " afterward in the necessary periods are healed by the fire . . . according to the amount of ingrained wickedness of each, the duration of his cure will be computed. This cure consists of the cleansing of his soul, and that cannot be achieved without an excruciating condition." [37]

In Saint Augustine also we find the idea of the intermediate state interpreted in unmistakably purgatorial terms. The interval between the death of the individual and the end of all things is used by God to purge the soul of the evil that clings to it because of its earthly misdeeds: " In this intermediate time, between the laying down and the receiving back of the body, souls will either be punished or rest in peace according to the deeds performed in their bodily existence." [38]

Thus the idea that the soul is a detachable part or substance, capable of existing independently of the body, was taken over from the " religious " anthropology and incorporated into Christian thought in the patristic period. This happened in spite of the fact that there is scarcely any Biblical basis for belief in the immortality of the soul in this sense, much less for its dualistic and puritanical implications. It happened for various reasons. The idea may have been adopted chiefly because it provided a plausible answer to the question about the supposed interval of time between death and resurrection, a question that may have been at least partly inspired by a misunderstanding of the nature of time.[39] In addition, the Fathers were no doubt impressed by the force of the arguments advanced by Greek philosophy to prove the immortality of the soul. And, finally, of course, the idea of an intermediate state gave the human being another chance to be purged of his sins before the last judgment. It was the development of this notion that led to the doctrine of purgatory, with all the superstitions and objectionable practices that eventually made up the purgatorial system and, in the end, furnished part of the immediate cause of the Reformation.

SAINT THOMAS AQUINAS

Saint Augustine and the Christian philosophers who succeeded him from the fifth to the twelfth centuries tended for the most part to rationalize the Christian faith in Platonic terms. They were particularly likely, therefore, to interpret man as consisting of two separate and distinct parts or substances, the body and the soul, more or less accidentally and unfortunately joined together.

In the thirteenth century, with the recovery of the Aristotelian works that, with the exception of the logic, had been long missing from Western thought, Saint Thomas Aquinas attempted to work out a Christian philosophy in terms of Aristotle rather than of Plato. And since Aristotle had developed his thought in opposition to Plato's *chōrismos* or dualism, Saint Thomas in constructing his theory of man was in a better position to remain faithful to the Biblical view that man is a unity, in whom the physical aspects are as essential as the psychical.

Aquinas began his anthropology by following Aristotle closely. Man is not a composite of two different substances, but rather a single unified substance. Every substance in nature has two aspects, its form (the structure that it shares with other things of the same class) and its matter (the actual stuff that makes it a particular thing). In vegetables, animals, and man, the form may be called the soul, and the matter the body. Soul and body are thus inseparable aspects of the same one substance and each requires the other in order to exist at all.

Saint Thomas insisted that the soul in man is simply the form of that same substance of which the matter is the body: " It belongs to the notion of a soul to be the form of the body." [40] The soul is nothing apart from the body of which it is the form, just as a pattern is nothing apart from that of which it is the pattern. Aquinas specifically criticized Plato and Saint Augustine for saying that man *is* a soul or " a soul making use of a body," for it is clear that " man is not only a soul but something composed of soul *and* body." [41]

Saint Thomas was fully aware of the soul's dependence on the body and of the extent to which the mental faculties are tied to their physiological bases. He recognized, in other words, the intimate interrelationship between the physical and the psychical. Thought, which is man's peculiar function, has to make use of sensations, and these sensations are received from the physical sense organs. This is one of the reasons for insisting that the body is essential to man: " The soul in a certain way requires the body for its operations." [42]

" It [the soul] has to gather knowledge from understanding things by way of the senses . . . and therefore the intellectual soul has to be endowed . . . with the power of sensing. Now the action of the senses is not performed without a corporeal instrument. Therefore the intellectual soul has to be united to a body which could be the fitting organ of sense." [43]

Thus Saint Thomas concluded that " the soul as a part of human nature has its natural perfection only as united to a body." [44] The soul is not loosely and accidentally inserted into a body, but is rather essentially and necessarily and (one would suppose) inextricably intermingled with the body. It is not the case that " its [the soul's] union with the body is accidental; for, on the contrary, such a union belongs to it according to the very character of its nature." [45]

This is a very strong statement of the view that the physical and psychical aspects of man's being are so completely interrelated and interdependent as to be inseparable. It is almost at the opposite pole from the dualism of the " religious " view. It fits in well with the Biblical account of man as a unified organism to which the body is essential, an account that culminates in, and is heavily underlined by, the declaration of the resurrection of the body.

The position reached by Saint Thomas at this point and the questions to which it gives rise are summarized by a sympathetic commentator as follows:

" We have seen that Saint Thomas rejected the Platonic-Augustinian view of the relation of soul to body and adopted the Aristotelian view of the soul as the form of the body, emphasizing the closeness of the union between the two. There is no *forma corporeitatis,* there is but one substantial form in man, the rational soul, which directly informs pure matter and is the cause of all human activities on the vegetative, sensitive, and intellectual levels: sensation is an act, not o the soul using a body, but of the *compositum;* we have no innate ideas, but the mind is dependent on sense-experience for its knowledge. The question arises, therefore, whether the closeness of the union between soul and body has not been so emphasized that the possible subsistence of the human soul apart from the body must be ruled out. In other words, is not the Aristotelian doctrine of the relation of soul to body incompatible with personal immortality? If one starts with the Platonic theory of the soul, immortality is assured, but the union of soul and body is rendered difficult to understand; whereas if one starts with the Aristotelian theory of the soul, it might seem that one has to sacrifice immortality, that the soul is so closely bound to the body that it cannot subsist apart from the body." [46]

This would indeed seem to be the conclusion to which the logic of both the Aristotelian and the Thomistic anthropology is driven. However, by the thirteenth century the doctrine of the immortality of the soul, in the Greek sense, had become so much a part of Christian thought that Saint Thomas could not bring himself to deny it. In order to maintain this belief he had, in the end, to return with Aristotle to dualism. In Aristotle, this relapse was due, first of all, to his view that reason in man not only distinguishes him from the rest of nature but is actually a spark of the divine and eternal Reason; and, secondly, to his belief that human reason, being divine in origin and nature, could by a supreme effort escape from the body and be reabsorbed into the Pure Form from which it came. In accepting these ideas, so foreign to the general tenor of his thinking, Aristotle was a victim of the tradition, deeply entrenched in Greek culture, that we have called the " religious " anthropology. Saint Thomas accepted the first of these beliefs in a modified version: it is reason that differentiates man from the animals and relates him to God. In fact, reason constitutes the image of God in man: " Man is said to be in the image of God by reason of his intellectual nature " [47]; and again: " To be in the image of God belongs only to the mind." [48] Thus the mind, once again, is cut off sharply from the body.

The way in which Saint Thomas distinguished the human from the animal soul also led him in the direction of dualism. The animal soul is capable of sensing, but it cannot on the basis of its sensations proceed to think. The human soul, while it must begin the quest for knowledge with sensations, is able to go on to form abstract ideas and, therefore, to think in complete independence of bodily sensations, as in mathematics and logic.

This argument, which is of course Platonic, is the main ground that Saint Thomas adduced to support his return to the old idea that the soul is capable of surviving the death of the body. He therefore maintained that the soul of man is the one case in nature of a form that can exist independent of matter. In his language this means that the soul is a " subsistent form ":

" The mind or intellect has essentially an operation [abstract thought] in which the body does not share. Now only that which subsists in itself can have an operation peculiar to itself; therefore the human soul is something subsistent." [49]

Now to say that the soul is a " subsistent form " is very nearly a contradiction in terms within the framework of the Thomistic categories. The word " subsistent " is derived from " substance," while " form " is regularly the form *of* some substance. To speak of a " subsistent form " is to suggest, against the grain of the whole system, that there is a form that is not an aspect of a substance but is itself a substance. He was led into this contradiction partly because he finally succumbed, like Aristotle before him, to the Greek glorification of reason at the expense of matter,[50] and partly because the Greek doctrine of the immortality of the soul, which he felt bound to accept, entailed the notion that the soul was a detachable part of human nature. Having arrived at the conclusion that the soul is a " subsistent form " and has independent being, he could go on to argue, in the familiar fashion of the old " religious " anthropology, that the soul is by its very nature incorruptible and not affected by the death of the body: " The intellectual principle that we call the human soul is incorruptible

. . . it is impossible for a subsistent form to cease to exist." [51]

These ideas which contradict a great deal that he had previously said about the soul involved Saint Thomas in serious difficulties. At times he seems obviously embarrassed as he struggles with them. For example, he had stated, quite unambiguously, that it belongs to the *very nature* of the human soul to be united to a body.[52] It would follow, then, that in its disembodied state, the " soul " is no longer a soul, properly speaking, at all; its " very nature " has changed. True, said Saint Thomas, " to be separated from the body is not in accord with its nature." Nevertheless, he could not give up the idea, and so he concluded lamely: " Nevertheless, it is possible for it to exist apart from the body." [53] We simply have to recognize, he said, that its mode of existence is then unnatural and incomplete; it awaits the recovery of its body at the last day.

Thus we arrive at the strange picture that is often called " the traditional Christian doctrine." It thinks, we are told,[54] " of simple immortality as a bare minimum, and portrays the discarnate soul as yearning for renewed union with the body." In actual fact, this is just the old " Orphic " idea of a detachable soul, now modified, not to say rendered finally ridiculous, by the notion that the separated soul is unhappy in this divorce and longs to be reunited with her " worse half."

Saint Thomas Aquinas, then, arrived in the end at his own version of body-soul dualism. It should be pointed out, however, that this dualism was not only modified but was also accompanied, as in most of the Church Fathers, by a " high " view of the body. There is little trace of that antiphysical bias that characterized the dualism of the Gnostic, Manichaean, and Neoplatonic type. The Thomistic ethics followed the moderate, eminently sensible, Aristotelian model, adding to the " cardinal " or Greek virtues the Christian or " theological " virtues of faith, hope, and love.

At the same time there was alongside the Thomistic synthesis a strong Neoplatonic tradition of long standing in medieval thought. This tradition not only advocated a more extreme form of body-soul dualism, including a tendency to regard the soul as divine, but also, as was normal in this line of thought, adopted a contemptuous and hostile attitude to the body. Such a philosophy was apt to lead to fanatical asceticism and to express itself in a repressive and otherworldly ethics. This Neoplatonic tradition in Christian thought enjoyed a revival in the fourteenth and fifteenth centuries. Its anthropology and ethics were prevalent and influential when the Protestant Reformers appeared on the scene.

APPENDIX TO CHAPTER III: IRENAEUS' CHILIASM

Irenaeus' eschatology is an example of "millenarianism" or "chiliasm." After the end of the world as we know it, there will be a period of one thousand years in which "the righteous" or "the saints" will rule over a renovated natural order. Most of the quotations from Irenaeus that we have given in the text refer to this millennial period. This "time of the Kingdom," however, is not, for Irenaeus, the ultimate destiny of the saints. It is a time of further progress and development toward perfection. This will culminate, apparently, in the full vision of God. "The Son will yield up his work to the Father" and God will be "all in all" (*Against Heresies,* V. 36.2).

Undoubtedly, the end of the present order is not the ultimate "end" for Irenaeus. There will be an intervening period in which both nature and human nature will be perfected. There is no indication, however, in Irenaeus that the return of all things to the Father will involve the annihilation of matter, any more than it will entail the obliteration of human persons. On the contrary, Irenaeus asserts more than once that the renovated earth of the millennium will remain "for ever" (*op. cit.,* V. 36.1, and IV. 28.2.). The fact is that while the millennium itself is described by Irenaeus in concrete and "materialistic" terms, the ultimate consummation is very vaguely conceived. It does not, however, appear to be thought of in a purely "spiritual" way.

It is significant of the "spiritualizing" tendencies of the Church of later centuries that the last five chapters of *Against Heresies,* in which Irenaeus' eschatology is outlined, were omitted, no doubt deliberately, and are now missing in most MSS. It is further significant of the assumptions of the Church in our day that millenarianism is usually associated with the " lunatic fringe," and that it has been left to the sects (like the Seventh Day Adventists and Jehovah's Witnesses) to preserve the " materialism " of the Biblical eschatology.

CHAPTER IV

The "Religious" View
in Reformation and
Modern Thought

WE HAVE SEEN how the "religious" anthropology, in a modified form, was incorporated into Christian thought by the early and medieval Christian philosophers. From this source it has passed into the whole Catholic tradition in Christianity. But Protestantism is by no means free of it. In fact, the Reformers took over from the Neoplatonism of the late medieval period a strong form of dualism, and it is well-known that in Calvinism the repressive, authoritarian ethics of the "religious" anthropology received its definitive statement. Indeed, this was the principal contribution of Protestantism to the modern version of this kind of anthropology.

We must proceed now to trace this development. We shall then examine the way in which the "religious" anthropology reappears in modern secular thought, first in the Renaissance writers and afterward, through Descartes, passing into one of the main streams of modern philosophy.

THE REFORMATION

The characteristic marks of the "religious" anthropology are its body-soul dualism, its hostility to the body, and its belief in the immortality of the detachable soul. In the Christian versions of this anthropology that we have so far encountered a desire to maintain the third doctrine leads to an assertion of the first, while adoption of the first, in turn, has a tendency to carry the second with it. The connection between belief in the immortality of the independent soul and a dualistic analysis of human nature is found again in the Reformers. But the repressive morality, as we shall see, has here a rather different derivation.

Martin Luther was by no means a systematic theologian or thinker. While in many well-known instances he made his position unmistakably clear, there are still a number of cases where it is difficult to be sure exactly where he stood. As far as his understanding of man is concerned, he appears at times unquestionably to have adopted an extreme dualism. "Man," he wrote, "has a twofold nature. According to the spiritual nature, which men call the soul, he is called spiritual or inner or new man; according to the bodily nature, which men call the flesh, he is called carnal or outward or old man." [1]

It is possible to interpret this passage in two different ways. In the sentences that follow he certainly seems to have been suggesting that the soul, even in this life, is so completely different and separate from the body that it cannot be affected by anything that the body does. This interpretation, indicating an extreme body-soul dualism of the Neoplatonic type, is borne out by his belief in the immortality of the separated soul, which he expressed by saying, quite unambiguously, "The soul may live without the body." [2] The dualistic implications are obvious. On this interpretation, Luther was confusing the Pauline antithesis between "the flesh" and "the spirit" (which is simply the antithesis between "the old man" and "the new man" and therefore implies no dualism [3]) with the Greek contrast of body and soul.

On the other hand, the fact that Luther in this passage rightly equated "the flesh" with "the old man" and "the spirit" with "the new man" shows that another interpretation is possible. By man's "twofold nature" Luther may have meant, not the difference between body and soul, but the distinction between man as sinful and unregenerate and man as justified and redeemed. This interpretation is borne out by another somewhat cryptic passage that seems to point in this direction: " There is another division of each of these three, body, soul, and spirit . . . into two parts [sic] which are called spirit and flesh. This is a division, *not of the nature of man, but of his qualities . . . All of these,* body, soul, and spirit, may be good or evil, that is, *may be spirit or flesh.*" [4] As a matter of fact, in spite of his remark already quoted, it is not even clear that he accepted the immortality of the soul in the Greek sense. For elsewhere he said, with characteristic vigor: " If now one would say, ' The soul of Abraham lives with God, his body lies here dead,' it would be a distinction which to my mind is mere rot! I will dispute it." [5] The truth is that Luther never worked out a definite anthropology, and his statements on the subject are not always consistent.

When we come to Calvin, however, there is no difficulty of interpretation. His dualism is unmistakable:

" Man is evidently composed of two substances, neither of which is so confounded with the other as not to retain its distinct nature . . . Wherefore, that is predicated separately of the soul which cannot at all be applied to the body. On the contrary, that is predicated of the body which is totally incompatible with the soul."

To be sure, he went on to soften this by pointing out that we ascribe things to " the whole man " that cannot properly be ascribed to either the body or the soul alone. But he concluded the passage on a clearly dualistic note: " Such forms of expression signify that there is in man one person composed of two distinct parts and that there are two different natures united in him to constitute one person." [6] Moreover, he argued for the immortality of the soul on the familiar Greek grounds. The soul of man is a " distinct substance" and its rational and moral faculties both prove its immortality and also constitute the image of God in man. [7]

It is not surprising, in view of this adoption of a Neoplatonic dualism, that a repressive ethics, the usual corollary of this doctrine, also reappeared and, in fact, received its definitive form in the Calvinist version of Reformed Christianity. What is surprising is that this kind of moralism should have so speedily emerged in Protestantism. For the Reformation was a revolt against the legalism and authoritarianism of late medieval Catholicism, and the major accusation against this kind of Catholicism was that it perverted Christianity into a religion of law like the kind of Judaism that Jesus and Paul attacked so vigorously. Luther regarded himself as in the great tradition of Jesus and Paul when he proclaimed the " liberty " of the Christian man over against the " law " of the Catholic Church, and when he insisted that " faith " and not " works " was the ground of the believer's justification.

It is undeniable that the late medieval Church maintained its authority over its members by constructing an intricate, legalistic system of works, fastings, penances, ritual observances, and detailed moral rules. Luther protested against the implication, clearly present, that a man could be saved by such things. At the same time he was anxious that his followers should not confuse liberty with license, or the Christian way of life with antinomianism. Ritual and rules have their place, but it should be recognized that their performance is the result and not the cause of our justification in the sight of God. Nothing we can *do,* can *earn* our salvation. It is God alone in Christ who has *done* something. And by his act we are redeemed. Apart from that, we are all alike miserable and powerless sinners upon whom the wrath of an omnipotent God is justly visited.

In this sharp contrast between the sinfulness and powerlessness of man and the holiness and omnipotence of God, we have the seeds of the Calvinist development. Zwingli and Calvin made it the foundation of their theology. Sinful man can do nothing whatever that retains the least vestige of goodness. Therefore, not even his faith, by which he is justified, can be his own. It too is the work of God, accomplished by him in those whom he has elected to salvation. This is all of a piece with Calvin's emphasis on the omnipotent will, rather than the love, of God. In harmony with this conception of God, the Christian life is no longer an expression of gratitude for God's forgiving love but simply a matter of rigid and unquestioning obedience to the will of God. Similarly, the Bible is interpreted, not in terms of the gospel of love, but as an absolutistic code of conduct dictated by an omnipotent and wrathful being.[8] And this code, as elaborated by Calvin, is both repressive and authoritarian. Its hostility to the natural pleasures of life is perhaps derived, as before, from body-soul dualism, but the authoritarian aspects of the system are to be explained in the light of Calvin's idea of God. Yet the question still remains: How does this return to repressive legalism in ethics fit in with the Reformers' doctrine of justification by faith and not by works and with the belief in predestination? The Calvinists' answer would be, first, that the elect still retain their sinful tendencies and therefore have to be subjected to rigorous discipline; secondly, that life in accordance with this strict, " puritanical " moral system is what God demands; and, thirdly, that such a life is the mark and not the ground of a man's election.

In any case, the practical effect is a return to a legalism and an authoritarianism far more rigorous than anything we find in medieval Catholicism. In fact, in the Calvinistic system, this kind of moralism is given its code and emerges as one typical expression of modern Protestantism. It survives powerfully down to the nineteenth century, by which time it has reached the extreme position of regarding pleasure as in itself wicked. Even in the twentieth century, Protestant denominations in this tradition often appear to spend most of their time and resources in combating alcohol, sex, and gambling. Thus Protestantism becomes identified, in the popular mind, with repressive moralism.

At the same time, in the face of the Protestant assertion of the right of private judgment, Catholicism began to stress, more strongly than ever, the need for implicit obedience to the authority of the Church, and by various means to extend its authoritarian control over every detail of the lives of its members. And often, for instance in Quebec, the ethics on which this control is based appears to be almost as " puritanical " as Calvinism.

So it comes about that modern Christianity, in both its Catholic and Protestant versions, not only becomes identified with a radical body-soul dualism, ultimately Greek in origin, but also combines the resulting suspicion of natural pleasures with a legalistic and authoritarian ethics similar to that of late Judaism. In other words, modern Christianity often manages to combine the worst features of both its Greek and its Hebrew inheritance.

Thus the attack that the Reformers made on the legalism and formalism of the late medieval Church did not have very fortunate results in the sphere of ethics. Their protests against the abuses of the purgatorial system did not have a much happier outcome, at any rate in the strictly theological realm. We should expect them to reject the idea of the intermediate state and to concentrate instead, as far as their teaching on the future life was concerned, on the Biblical doctrine of the general resurrection at the last day. This was what Luther, for the most part, did:

" As for purgatory, no place in Scripture makes mention thereof, neither must we anyway allow it . . . The bounds of purgatory stretch not beyond this world; for here in this life, the upright, good and godly Christians are well and soundly scourged and purged." [9]

If anyone is curious as to what happens after death, Luther's advice was that we should answer as Christ did to the disciples who

" were without doubt just as curious. ' He that believeth in me, though he were dead, yet shall he live.' Abraham lives. God is the God of the living. If now one would say, ' The soul of Abraham lives with God, his body lies here dead,' it would be a distinction which to my mind is mere rot! I will dispute it. One must say: ' The whole Abraham, the entire man, lives.' " [10]

Luther usually assumed that the dead are " asleep " or " at rest." [11] It is not easy to see just how this is to be reconciled with the last quotation. And in another place Luther went even farther toward accepting the idea of an intermediate state. In discussing the question of prayers for the dead, he said we know so little about their condition that we should pray, if at all, in this fashion: " Dear God, if the departed souls be in a state that they may yet be helped, then I pray that thou wouldst be gracious." [12] This is somewhat reminiscent of the skeptic's prayer: " O God, if there be a God, save my soul, if I have a soul." But it shows that Luther had not altogether abandoned the notion of the soul's disembodied existence; as we have previously seen, he stated explicitly, in one place, that " the soul may live without the body." [13]

Calvin also, in what he had to say about the future life, emphasized the resurrection of the body and the last things. But he accepted, much more definitely than Luther, the idea of the immortality of the separated soul and some kind of intermediate state:

" It is a brutish error to represent the spirit, formed after the image of God, as a fleeting breath which animates the body only during this perishable life, and to annihilate the temple of the Holy Spirit; in short, to despoil that part of us, in which Divinity is eminently displayed and the characters of immortality are conspicuous, of this property . . . Unless our souls survive our bodies, what is it that is present with God when separated from the body? " [14]

There is an intermediate state, then, in which the separated soul awaits the recovery of its body. This is indistinguishable from the patristic and medieval attempt to combine the Greek and Biblical views on man's ultimate destiny. But Calvin went on to warn against the purgatorial elaborations of the medieval Church:

" Overcurious inquiry respecting their intermediate state is neither lawful nor useful. Many persons exceedingly perplex themselves by discussing what place they occupy, and whether they already enjoy the glory of heaven or not. But it is folly and presumption to push our inquiries on unknown things beyond what God permits us to know.

The Scripture declares that Christ is present with them, and receives them into paradise, where they enjoy consolation, and that the souls of the reprobate endure the torments which they have deserved; but it proceeds no farther." [15]

Here Calvin seems to have been confusing the ideas of heaven and hell, which are eschatological concepts in the New Testament, with ideas that pertain to the intermediate state. This foreshadows the later developments in Protestantism in which, first the two sets of ideas are completely fused, and then, finally, the notion of hell is dropped and heaven alone remains — a place to which, it is optimistically expected, virtually all souls ascend at death.

We are now in a position to summarize the development of Christian anthropology from the second to the sixteenth centuries. The Church Fathers had before them, on the one hand, the Bible, which, as we shall see, is remarkably free of the typical assumptions of the " religious " view of man. On the other hand, they had to preach to a Hellenistic world in which an exaggerated form of " Orphism " prevailed. Their resulting anthropology was a mixture of Biblical and Greek ideas. They added to the New Testament doctrine of the resurrection of the body the idea of an intermediate state in which the soul exists apart from the body, awaiting its recovery at the end. But they insisted on a generally " high " view of the body that was in sharp contrast to the antiphysical bias of the prevailing pagan philosophies. The doctrine of the intermediate state, however, since it involved the idea of a separate existence of the soul, meant that the Biblical assumption of the unity of man's nature had to be surrendered in favor of the " religious " view of man as a composite of two different substances, the one essentially incorruptible and immortal and the other intrinsically perishable and earthy.

Saint Thomas Aquinas struggled harder than any of his predecessors to avoid a two-substance theory of human nature but, in the end, because of the strength of the Greek idea of immortality,

he was forced to concede that the soul is a separable and therefore distinct entity. Finally, the Reformers very largely took
over the medieval anthropology and in Calvinism a repressive
and authoritarian ethics was elaborated in a more extreme form
than had ever appeared before in orthodox Christian thought.

With this review of the history of Christian anthropology before us, it is impossible to deny that certain elements of the " religious " view of man have played a prominent part in Christian
thought. In view of the facts, it is difficult to see how J. V. L.
Casserley can say that " any competent theologian " would agree
with Fred Hoyle that there is " no part of man, called his ' mind '
[which] has within it some inherent property which gives it
power to survive the dissolution of the body." [16] It would seem
to be somewhat drastic to exclude Irenaeus, Gregory of Nyssa,
Saint Augustine, Saint Thomas Aquinas, John Calvin, and many
others from the class of " competent theologians." They all unquestionably believed that one part of human nature has the
" power to survive the dissolution of the body." We may believe that the dualism that this view entails is both un-Biblical in
origin and mistaken in fact, but we have to concede that it has
been adopted by many Christian theologians. The unfortunate
fact is that for centuries some aspects of the " religious " anthropology have been sold under the Christian label.

THE RENAISSANCE

The fifteenth and sixteenth centuries witnessed not only a great
reformation on the ecclesiastical level but also momentous changes
in the whole cultural and intellectual atmosphere of the Western
world. These changes are commonly grouped together under the
name "Renaissance." For this revolutionary movement was regarded as a rebirth of the pre-Christian Greek spirit of free, unfettered inquiry, in contrast to medieval thought which was
alleged to have been in bondage to the dogmas of the Church.

One of the watchwords of the Renaissance was "freedom" —

freedom from the moral and intellectual domination of the Church, freedom from the economic shackles of the feudal system, and freedom from the political tyranny of the Holy Roman Empire. Now the way in which the Renaissance thinkers, by and large, interpreted the concept of freedom was of great importance for the future of Western thought and of immediate relevance to our thesis. The Renaissance tended to identify freedom with man's alleged ability *to choose anything he wants*. And this unlimited and unconditioned freedom of choice was thought to be exercised by man's completely independent rational soul or mind.

We can see how these ideas were one aspect of the Renaissance insistence on man's absolute autonomy and the assumption that man can make himself anything he chooses. These ideas, constituting what we shall call the " libertarian " conception of freedom, are important because they become firmly planted in the modern Western tradition, and they are relevant to our thesis because they arise in conjunction with an extreme Neoplatonic body-soul dualism. If a repressive, moralistic ethics is the special contribution of the Reformation to the " religious " anthropology, this libertarian conception of freedom is the peculiar contribution of the Renaissance.

We have seen how the revival of Neoplatonism in the late medieval period influenced the Reformers. In the Renaissance writers we find again the old idea that the soul, especially in its intellectual capacities, is completely separate and distinct from the body. This dualism here leads on to the idea that the soul is *free* in its choices and decisions, while the body is under the compulsion of instincts and appetites. Thus Marsilio Ficino, a typical fifteenth century Renaissance philosopher, wrote:

"Intellect . . . guides its own motion according to free choice. Sense, however, when reason does not resist, is always driven by the instinct of nature . . . The beginning of choice does not depend on the body . . . It is seen from this that reason is never subjected to bodily things in its motion, because in its speculations it transcends

bodily things . . . Therefore, we say that intellect is much less subjected to any corporeal substance, in essence and in life . . . Moreover, sense is limited to corporeal objects; the intellect, in its inmost
action, frees itself from all corporeal things, seeing that in its essence
and life it has not been submerged." [17]

The familiar idea that the rational soul is capable of activities
that are completely independent of the body is here used to prove
not so much its immortality but rather its freedom — where freedom is interpreted as unrestricted ability to choose. The choices
of the independent soul are not conditioned in any way by the
compulsions that obtain in the body.

The extremes to which these ideas can be taken are illustrated
by Giovanni Pico, a friend and follower of Ficino, who used this
conception of the completely free and unconditioned soul to argue
that man is altogether independent of nature and has the unlimited power to make himself into anything he likes. He pictured
the Creator addressing Adam in the following words:

" ' Neither a fixed abode nor a form that is thine own nor any function peculiar to thyself have we given thee, Adam, to the end that,
according to thy judgment, thou mayest have and possess what abode,
what form, and what functions thou thyself shalt desire. The nature
of all other beings is limited and constrained within the bounds of
laws prescribed by us. Thou, *constrained by no limits, in accordance
with thine own free will,* in whose hand we have placed thee, shalt
ordain for thyself the limits of thy nature . . . so that with *freedom
of choice* and with honor, as though *the maker and molder of thyself,*
thou mayest fashion thyself in whatever shape thou shalt prefer. Thou
shalt have the power to degenerate into the lower forms of life, which
are brutish. Thou shalt have the power, out of thy soul's judgment,
to be reborn into the higher forms, which are divine.' O supreme
generosity of God the Father, O highest, most marvelous felicity of
man! To him it is granted *to have whatever he chooses, to be whatever he wills.*" [18]

This is a typical Renaissance view of man, and one that was to
have profound influence on modern thought. It is the pretentious,
titanic form of modern humanism. Man is separate from, and

master of, the rest of nature, not only because of the rationality but also by virtue of the complete autonomy and independence of his soul. This is the libertarian conception of freedom, in which freedom is interpreted in terms of unrestricted and unlimited choice.

There was, however, another strain in Renaissance thinking that was to have very different, but no less important, consequences. Pietro Pomponazzi,[19] in the same fifteenth century, followed the Aristotelian anthropology to its logical conclusions. Body and soul are inseparably united and utterly interdependent; therefore, both the immortality of the soul and the freedom of the will must be categorically denied. In this, Pomponazzi was more Aristotelian than Saint Thomas Aquinas or even Aristotle himself. He gave a completely naturalistic account of man. Thus, as Ficino and Pico, in a certain sense, anticipated the seventeenth century philosopher Descartes, so Pomponazzi, though his anthropology had a very different philosophical basis, anticipated the seventeenth century materialist Thomas Hobbes.

MODERN PHILOSOPHY

Between the fifteenth and seventeenth centuries, between Pico and Pomponazzi on the one hand and Hobbes and Descartes on the other, an immensely important development began to take place. One result of the new spirit of unfettered inquiry was the birth of modern science. The great scientific pioneers, Copernicus, Kepler, Galileo, and the rest, began to investigate the nature of the physical universe, not in terms of the old Aristotelian philosophy of nature, so long accepted as the last word, but rather by means of careful and continuous observation of the facts as they presented themselves to unprejudiced investigation. On the basis of observation, hypotheses were made. These hypotheses were tested by deducing their consequences and then returning to observation and experiment in order to determine whether the consequences, which should have followed if the hypotheses were true, did in fact occur. The use of this empirical method led the sixteenth and seventeenth century scientists more and more to the conclusion that the physical universe operated in the fashion of a great machine, the motion of which could be quantitatively measured and expressed in mathematical laws of motion. This development was in principle completed by Isaac Newton, with his formulation of the mechanical laws of motion and the principle of gravitation. The whole physical universe appeared to have been completely explained in quantitative and mechanical categories.

The pioneer scientists themselves restricted this type of explanation to the nonhuman physical world and, in fact, to its inanimate aspects. Mathematical physics, for them, had nothing to say about living organisms, much less about man. But very soon, indeed in the seventeenth century itself, philosophers appeared who began to transform the conclusions of the new science into metaphysical, all-inclusive doctrines by which they attempted to explain the whole of reality, including man himself. Hobbes and Gassendi are the names that are associated with the resulting mechanistic materialism. These philosophers maintained that everything that exists is nothing but matter in motion in accordance with fixed mechanical laws. The idea of spirit or soul in the sense of immaterial substance is simply a contradiction in terms, like "bodiless body." Human thought and human behavior, commonly attributed to the rational and free soul, are actually the products, like everything else, of matter and the mechanical laws that govern it.

In this view, human thought is simply the matter of the physical brain set in motion by stimuli from the external world. Human actions are the results of appetites and aversions arising from the pleasures and pains that are caused by the impact of external motion upon the internal motion of the body; what we regard as a free choice of the will, by virtue of which we perform a deliberate act, is nothing but the last appetite or aversion that happens to precede the overt bodily movement. In other words, there is no need to postulate either an independent reason to account for human thought or a free will to account for human behavior. Everything in man can be fully explained in terms of the body and the mechanical laws of motion. The existence of the soul, in any sense whatever, is denied.

It was a great misfortune that this kind of crude materialism should have set the tone for the whole modern attack on body-soul dualism. The grossness and the oversimplification of the Hobbes-Gassendi theory were objectionable in the extreme alike to the Christian and to the sensitive humanist. This type of materialism was met, therefore, by a reformulation of the old dualistic anthropology, in a version that was meant to do justice both to the new science and also to the conviction that man was more than a highly complicated machine.

The most typical and influential answer to the Hobbes-Gassendi thesis was worked out by the seventeenth century French philosopher, René Descartes. This answer attempted both to embrace what the new science had discovered about the nature of matter and also to satisfy the "religious" insistence that man possessed an immortal soul. When the choice lay between Hobbes and Descartes, it was natural, therefore, that the Christian should choose Descartes, and that the Cartesian anthropology should enter strongly into modern Christian thought.

What Descartes did was to combine Hobbes's mechanistic materialism with the Renaissance conception of the free, independent soul. He divided reality into two distinct kinds of substance: extended substance (*res extensa*) — matter, and thinking substance (*res cogitans*) — mind. He then proceeded to explain the whole realm of *res extensa* in terms of the mechanistic category. Moreover, he included in this type of explanation not only inorganic matter (the subject of Newtonian physics) but also all living things, even the higher animals and the *bodies* of men. Everything in this sphere could be exhaustively explained by the mechanical laws of motion. This explanation of living organisms, including human bodies, in entirely mechanistic terms was justified by reference to Harvey's new theory of the circulation of the blood.[20] This theory suggested to Descartes that the Newtonian laws operated within living bodies and accounted for their unconscious motions.

In order to meet the obvious objections to this application of quantitative and mechanical principles to the nature of man, Descartes postulated a second kind of substance in man called "soul" or "mind." Soul is a simple, indivisible, immaterial substance "whose whole essence consists in thinking."[21] And "thinking" here covers all conscious states, including willing, imagining, and desiring.

For Descartes, then, man is a composite of two entirely different substances, a body and a mind. The human body, like the whole being of the animal, is simply a complicated piece of machinery. Its behavior can be completely described in terms of mechanical reflexes; its movements flow from the arrangements of its various parts in exactly the same way that the movements of a clock follow from the arrangements of its wheels and weights:

> "The motion which I have now explained follows as necessarily from the very arrangement of the parts . . . as does the motion of a clock from the power, the situation and shape of its counterweights and wheels."[22]

"The human body," said Descartes, is "a machine made by the hands of God."[23]

The human mind, however, in this view, is entirely different from and independent of the body. Descartes's argument, calculated to establish this as a fact, is well known. I can doubt, he said, the reality of everything without exception. But the one thing I cannot doubt is the fact that I am doubting. If it were not for this fact, then I could doubt my own existence; because of this fact, I know that I exist. But the act of doubting is an act of consciousness, an act of thought. Therefore, it is the fact that I am thinking that alone establishes my own existence: *Cogito, ergo sum.* One of the points that this argument was intended to prove is that thinking occurs in complete independence of the body:

" I observed that I could suppose that I had no body and that there was no world nor any place in which I might be; but that I could not therefore suppose that I was not; and that, on the contrary, from the very circumstance that I thought to doubt of the truth of other things, it most clearly and certainly followed that I was; . . . I thence concluded that I was a substance whose whole essence or nature consists only in thinking, and which, that it may exist, has need of no place *nor is dependent on any material thing;* so that 'I,' that is to say, *the mind* by which I am what I am, is *wholly distinct from the body,* and is even more easily known than the latter, and is such that though the latter were not, it would still continue to be all that it is." [24]

According to Descartes, it follows from the mind's complete independence of the body, first, that the mind cannot be derived from and developed out of matter but must be created separately by God, and, so to speak, added externally by the Creator: ". . . it [the soul] could by no means be educed from the power of matter . . . but . . . must be expressly created " [25]; and, secondly, it follows that the soul can survive the body and is immortal: ". . . the soul is of a nature wholly independent of the body and . . . consequently it is not liable to die with the latter; and, finally, because no other causes are observed capable of destroying it, we are naturally led thence to judge that it is immortal." [26]

This is the conception of man that has been stigmatized by Gilbert Ryle as the theory of " the ghost in the machine." [27] At first glance it seems almost identical with the Greek view, but on second thought it is clearly an even more extreme form of dualism. For the Greek and medieval philosophers the soul was not only the intellectual principle but also the principle of life; it was the vital principle that animates all living things, including plants and animals. Thus both Aristotle and Saint Thomas Aquinas held that there are vegetable and animal souls as well as rational souls, and that the latter include all that the former possess. The point is that according to the older view there is a vital, organic principle that makes all living things quite different from mechanically moving, inorganic matter. But for Descartes, plants and animals — the organic in general — are not differentiated from inorganic matter but are to be explained, in the same way as the latter, by references to the Newtonian mechanical laws of motion. Moreover, the human body is this kind of thing; it is just a complicated, clocklike mechanism. It follows that the soul or mind, to which reason and freedom belong, cannot even be thought of in Augustinian terms as present in every part of the body but must be an entirely separate and distinct thing.

This account surrendered to mechanics a great deal more than had ever been done before, except by the outright materialists of the Hobbesian type. By handing over all animal behavior and all man's physical behavior to mechanical explanation, it actually assisted the tendency, which it was meant to resist, to explain the whole of human life in this way.

Cartesian dualism also rendered much more difficult, and indeed set for subsequent thought, the problem of accounting for the undoubted fact of body-mind interaction. If body and mind are so entirely different and independent, certain questions immediately arise: First, how can the mind ever bridge the gap that exists between itself and the external world in such a way that it can be said to "know" the external world? Secondly, how can decisions of the mind be carried out in movements of the body? And, thirdly, how can conditions in the body affect the mental dispositions? Descartes "answered" the first question by postulating intermediate links between the mind and the external world in the shape of "ideas"; the mind receives "ideas" from the external world and these "ideas" represent or picture the real nature of the world. He "answered" the second and third questions by postulating another intermediate link, this time the pineal gland. The pineal gland is part of the physical constitution, but the soul can act upon it, inclining it this way and that, thus directing units of energy, called " animal spirits," to particular motor-nerves; in this way, the mind's orders are executed in appropriate bodily movements.

Descartes also utilized his conception of the independent soul, in Renaissance fashion, to account for the fact that man is capable of free, purposive actions in contrast to the mechanically determined behavior of matter. The Hobbes-Gassendi type of materialism produced an anthropology that was unacceptable not only because of the difficulty it encountered in satisfactorily explaining human consciousness, but also because it entailed a flat denial of human freedom in any sense whatever. Descartes accepted a mechanical determinism for the activities of the body but claimed that the soul, being completely independent of the body, was exempt from the laws that govern it. The mind is perfectly free to choose any ends or purposes it likes; through the medium of the pineal gland it directs the body in the execution of these purposes.

Thus Descartes reaffirmed the libertarian interpretation of freedom, first enunciated in the fifteenth century by Ficino and Pico. According to this view, freedom is the power, exercised by the independent soul, to choose anything it decides on: it is a capacity of free choice, uncoerced, unlimited, and unconditioned by any factors whatsoever. Such a conception of freedom had never appeared before, with the possible exception of that of Epicureanism. When the question of man's free will first began to be discussed, as such, in the third century B.C., it was advocated by the Epicureans alone. The Stoics denied it and argued that true freedom was found in submission to the laws of universal reason. The medieval Christian philosophers had given a limited place to freedom of choice, but recognized that the higher freedom could be achieved only by acting in accordance with the will of God. The Reformers denied that man's will was free; it was *enslaved* either to the devil or to God, and only in the latter case was it proper to speak of freedom.[28] But in Descartes, the champion of man's spiritual status and freedom against the crude materialism and determinism of Hobbes, freedom became identified with unlimited freedom to choose, that is to say, with the libertarian conception of freedom. This interpretation here entered into the Western mind, including the mind of modern, liberal Protestantism.

It is only in terms of this novel definition of freedom that we can understand the tremendous emphasis on private judgment, individualism, and free enterprise, so typical not only of liberal Protestantism but also of the philosophy of capitalism and liberal democracy in general in modern Western civilization. But what is even more relevant to our purpose to notice is that libertarianism was now added to dualism in the " religious " anthropology. The great misfortune was that the Christian conviction of man's freedom and spiritual dignity became bound up with dualism and libertarianism, while the attack on these doctrines was carried on chiefly by an oversimplified materialism that altogether denied the spirit and the freedom of man.

The great problem that Descartes's radical dualism bequeathed to subsequent thought was how to account for the obvious interaction and interrelationship of mind and body. If mind and body are two entirely separate and self-sufficient substances, how can the one exert any causal efficacy on the other; how is it that the intentions of the mind are translated so effortlessly and immediately into bodily behavior; and how is it that mental states produce bodily symptoms? Conversely, how is it that the condition of the body so clearly affects the mental disposition, and so on?

Leibniz, another seventeenth century philosopher, introduced the strange conception of " pre-established harmony " to answer such questions. God in his creation, he said, has so arranged it that " each substance, following its own law, falls in with what the other requires and thus the activities of the one follow or accompany the activities and changes of the other."²⁹ The illustration that Leibniz himself used was that the body and soul are like two clocks that are perfectly synchronized, due to the accuracy with which they were originally made. The question of the mind's free, purposive behavior as contrasted with the mechanical activity of the body was answered in the same way:

" Souls act in accordance with the laws of final causes [ends], through their desires, purposes, and means. Bodies act in accordance with the laws of efficient causes or of motion [mechanically]. The two realms, that of efficient causes [mechanism] and that of final causes [purpose], are in harmony each with the other" ³⁰

because God has ordained that it should be so. This theory of pre-established harmony is only slightly less implausible than the " occasionalism " of Malebranche, who suggested that God continually interposes to bring it about that the activities of mind and body correspond.

In the same century Spinoza used his theory of absolute monism to solve the same problem. In his view there is ultimately only one reality — the Absolute — which may be called God or Nature; and only one set of events — the events that take place in the life of the Absolute. The Absolute has, however, as two of its attributes, thought (mind) and extension (body). We apprehend the events in the life of the Absolute either under the attribute of thought or under the attribute of extension. But since there is actually only one set of events in reality, it follows that the order and connection of events we apprehend under the one attribute will be precisely the same as the order and connection we apprehend under the other. There will be a necessary and inevitable correspondence between mind and body. Similarly, what we regard as mechanical causation in the material mode we regard as teleological or purposive causation in the mental mode. This theory of Spinoza is entirely dependent on his rather complicated metaphysics and can be fully understood, if at all, only in that context. It is perhaps more easily intelligible in the form of the nineteenth century theory known as "psychophysical parallelism." This view held that the same reality that manifests itself subjectively for consciousness as an idea in the mind shows itself objectively for sense-perception as a physical process in the body.

In this brief survey of the seventeenth century thought, we seem to have been traveling farther and farther away from common sense. It is a relief to turn to the philosophy of Great Britain that received its clearest expression at the end of the same century in the work of John Locke. Locke's philosophy is relevant to our thesis because he began the critical examination of the concept of substance which is obviously fundamental in most forms of body-soul dualism. It is when body and soul are thought of as more or less self-sufficient substances that dualism appears in its most extreme forms.

Locke was an empiricist and believed that all knowledge comes from experience. Now it is clear that we are not directly acquainted with substance in sense-experience. What we perceive through our senses are various sensible qualities, like colors, tastes, sounds, smells, and shapes. We also discover in experience that certain specific qualities regularly occur together, and we report that we see, for example, "a table." But a little reflection reveals that what we actually observe is a certain set of sensible qualities. We *infer,* but do not observe, that they belong to the same thing — the table itself, the material substance. Thus the substance itself is never directly observed. It is an inferred support of qualities. The same is true of the substance we call the soul. What we are directly aware of in introspection is a number of ideas, feelings, states of mind, and so on. We *infer,* but do not introspect, that they belong to the same thing, the self, the mental substance. Thus, from the strictly empirical point of view, we have to admit that material and mental substances are objects of inference and not of direct experience. Locke recognized that for empiricism these inferences are somewhat hazardous but he nevertheless held that they were justified. He therefore continued to believe in the existence of these two kinds of substance and remained a body-soul dualist.

It was not long, however, before his eighteenth century successors took his line of reasoning to its logical conclusion. Bishop Berkeley denied that there were any sound reasons for postulating material substances as the unperceived supports of perceived qualities. There are no material "things" or substances, only collections of sense-qualities or ideas. But though he rejected the existence of material substance, Berkeley, rather oddly (perhaps because he was a bishop), retained the notion of spiritual substances or souls. Reality consists of spiritual substances, or minds, and their ideas.

This was obviously only a halfway house on the journey of eighteenth century empiricism. David Hume went the whole way. He argued that if all knowledge is derived from what we actually observe, it follows, first, that all we are entitled to say about a material "thing" is that it consists of sense-qualities or "impressions," and, secondly, that all we are entitled to say about the self is that it is "nothing but a bundle or collection of different perceptions, which succeed each other with an inconceivable rapidity, and are in perpetual flux and movement." [31] So, with Hume, we arrive at a position of complete skepticism about the existence of any substances at all, either physical or mental.

By the end of the eighteenth century, then, there were four distinct "solutions" of the body-mind problem: (*a*) the extreme body-soul dualism of Descartes, developed by Malebranche, Leibniz, and Christian von Wolff into a philosophy of dogmatic rationalism; (*b*) the mechanistic materialism of Hobbes and Gassendi, expounded by people like Condillac and d'Holbach; (*c*) the psychophysical parallelism of Spinoza, based on absolute monism; and (*d*) the complete skepticism of Hume.

This was the situation when Kant appeared and attempted, by

means of his " Copernican revolution," to reconcile the opposing views. It is impossible to summarize the Kantian philosophy; in fact, there are some who believe that it is impossible to explain it at all. We shall confine ourselves to certain points that are relevant to our purpose. Kant distinguished between reality as it appears to us — the " phenomenal " world — and reality as it is in itself — the " noumenal " world. Science and theoretical reason in general are restricted to the phenomenal world. This world is constituted partly by Hume's impressions or sense-qualities caused by " things in themselves " (the noumenal), and partly by forms and categories provided by the mind. These forms and categories are the means by which the mind organizes (and cannot avoid organizing) the sense-impressions that come from external reality. Substance and causality are two of these categories. Thus impressions are brought together to make up substances, and substances are related to each other in cause and effect series. It is the mind, however, and not reality as it is in itself, that furnishes these categories. But the mind is not normally aware that it is engaged in this kind of collecting and relating activity. It does it on a (so to speak) superconscious level, with the result that, for empirical observation, reality *appears to us* as already constituted by substances related in causal series. This is the way in which the mind *must* think its experience. Thus substances and causal relations belong to the world as it appears to us (the phenomenal world) but not to reality as it is in itself (the noumenal world).

This is true, Kant argued, not only of material substances, bodies, but also of mental or spiritual substances, souls. In so far as we think of the soul as a mental substance, as an object of introspection, that is to say as a kind of " thing," it belongs only to the phenomenal world and not to reality itself. The soul in this sense is simply a " phenomenon," in the technical sense; or, as we should now say, it is the *psyche* as science studies it. Science and theoretical reason cannot take us beyond this phenomenal level.

Nevertheless, we *can* get beyond it. We can get beyond the

phenomenal world through our moral experience or by means of what Kant calls *practical* reason. In our moral experience, according to Kant, we are aware of an absolute obligation to a universal moral law; we are aware that we " ought " to act in such and such a way. Now if I know that I ought to act in a certain way, this implies that I am able to act in a different way: " I ought, therefore I can." In other words, the validity of moral experience carries with it the reality of human freedom. But freedom is not found in the phenomenal world where causality, as we have seen, necessarily reigns supreme. Our awareness of freedom, therefore, takes us beyond the phenomenal world into noumenal reality, into reality as it is in itself. And this freedom belongs to a self which is not the substantial soul of the phenomenal world. This is the true self, the real " I "; it is not a " thing " or a substance accessible to introspection; in the language that we shall use later,[32] " it " is not an *object* at all, but a *subject*.

Kant accomplished a considerable *tour de force* in this treatment of the body-soul problem, but he left many questions still unanswered. On the phenomenal level we are left with the phenomenal body and soul as two distinct substances, and their interrelationship has not yet been explained. It is probable that he meant to indicate an answer along the lines of Spinoza and psychophysical parallelism. However that may be, Kant's most interesting contribution, from our point of view, was his suggestion that selfhood is not to be considered in terms of substance, as though the soul were a kind of *thing,* somewhat like a physical thing only more refined. It is this kind of thinking, which perhaps unconsciously conceives of the soul as analogus to a physical substance, that creates so many difficulties in this field. It is a profound mistake to think of the soul as a kind of substance, simply differing in certain respects from other substances, a soul-substance rather than a body-substance. Kant seems to have been suggesting, in opposition to this view, that selfhood is actually a certain *status of being,* rather than a *part* of human nature. This is a clue that we shall later pursue.[33]

The modern form of the " religious " anthropology is, in many respects, a more extreme version than any of the ancient and medieval varieties. In the first place, the ascetic and rigoristic tendencies of this view of man were intensified in the repressive and authoritarian ethics of Calvin. Secondly, Descartes's philosophy contained a body-soul dualism in some ways more radical than any of the earlier types. And finally, the Renaissance interpretation of man added to this set of ideas a libertarian conception of freedom that was virtually without precedent in Western thought.

The denial of man's spirit and freedom, and the rejection of the objectivity of values, which were to be made with increasing force throughout the nineteenth and twentieth centuries, have to be understood in the light of these implausible ideas of the soul, the free will, and the moral obligation of man. As long as these were the only available alternatives, it is not surprising that naturalism, determinism, and relativism gained many adherents. Moreover, the scientific evidence, which was now piling up, both definitely refuted the " religious " anthropology and also appeared to confirm these doctrines that lay at the opposite extreme.

PART TWO

The "Scientific" View of Man

CHAPTER V

The Scientific Evidence

KANT'S DEATH in 1804 brings us to the beginning of the nineteenth century. It was in this century that the various sciences began to concern themselves more and more with the study of human nature. It is time now to turn to the evidence that comes from these sources.

So far we have contented ourselves with expounding the doctrines of the "religious" anthropology in their various forms. At the same time we have strongly implied that, in our opinion, this view of man is both un-Biblical and false. We have not yet provided much ground to support this opinion. What we believe to be the genuine Biblical anthropology will be set forth in detail subsequently.[1] As for the alleged falsity of the view of man that we have been discussing hitherto, it is the modern sciences, more than anything else, that have furnished the clinching evidence against, and the unanswerable objections to, the old Greek way of looking at man and his destiny. Scientific investigation seems to have proved conclusively that body-soul dualism, rigoristic moralism, and libertarianism constitute an entirely false mythology and are responsible for much unnecessary human distress.

Greek thought, motivated by a very proper desire to differentiate man from the rest of nature, went too far and exaggerated the difference between nature and man. What modern science has done, operating within its naturalistic limitations, is to show that man is much more intimately involved in nature than the older view had supposed. Science has proved that there is a vast array of natural, material conditions that play a large part in shaping human life, including such factors as thought, choice, morality, and character which were formerly ascribed to the independent soul. It has now been established that all these factors that make up a man's being are dependent to a great degree on their physical and material bases. It is not possible, in view of the concrete evidence, to think of man as consisting of two separate parts or substances. Science has taught us to look at man as a unified psychosomatic organism.

In the scientific view, man is a unitary being in whom the physical and psychical aspects are so completely interrelated and overlapping that no clear lines can be drawn between them, except more or less arbitrarily for purposes of analysis. Dualism hears its death knell sounded. And if dualism has to be abandoned, we can no longer suppose that the soul is a detachable part that can survive bodily death by itself. The old doctrine of the immortality of the separated soul must now itself be gently ushered into the place of departed spirits. Similarly, we can no longer regard the body as a second separable part of man, the source of all temptation and sin, which must be sternly suppressed. Repressive moralism is given its obituary notice. Finally, the idea of freedom as the capacity for unconditioned and unlimited choice, residing in the independent soul, is also doomed to oblivion.

What is the scientific evidence that seems to point so strongly in this direction? We can divide it into three parts, corresponding on the one hand to three distinct types of science, the physical, the social, and the psychological, and on the other to three main sets of material conditions in human life, the physiological, the sociological, and the psychological.

THE PHYSICAL SCIENCES

The first set of material factors that clearly condition human nature are the strictly physical. The most important of these factors are studied by the biological sciences. Perhaps we should mention, first of all, the fact of *evolution*. This fact establishes the unity and kinship of all life from the lowest to the highest forms. The proliferation of species of living things, including the emergence of the human species, is not the result of a sudden, once-and-for-all act of creation, but of a long, slow process of differentiation. The living things best adapted by nature to their environment survive in the struggle for existence. The survivors reproduce offspring that inherit the same characteristics, and thus species become established. The offspring, however, differ from their parents and from one another by virtue of variations. Individuals receiving favorable variations will, in turn, tend to win out over their less favored brothers and thus survive and reproduce. Favorable variations will accumulate through successive generations until eventually descendants will be produced that are so different from their forebears that they have to be regarded as a new species. The whole process appears to be explicable in terms of adaptation, variations, and natural selection.

The relevant point is that man appeared on the scene in the course of this natural process. This means, among other things, that he is intimately related to the higher animals and to the rest of nature. As a matter of fact, we share many things with our ape relatives: the same kind of skeleton, sense organs, instincts, the same methods of breathing, eating, and reproducing. And if these factors in man's nature are so similar to those of the higher animals, it is probable that human activities, like thinking, willing, acting purposefully and morally, are also evolutionary developments out of more rudimentary animal forms of the same kind of thing.

In other words, man does not differ sharply and radically from the higher animals, but only by virtue of the number and nature of his variations and by reason of more fully developed forms of tendencies that are incipient throughout the process. This kind of evidence is plainly fatal to a " spiritual " anthropology which postulates the insertion at some point of an independent soul to account for man's higher faculties and to distinguish him from the rest of nature.

A second contribution that physical science makes to the understanding of the material basis of the whole of human life is the elucidation of the part that is played by *the physiological nervous system and brain* in sensation, thought, and consciousness in general. As early as the second century A.D., some of these facts were known to Galen and, as we have seen, to a few of the Church Fathers. But it was only in the nineteenth century that physiology succeeded in describing, with something like completeness, the whole network of physical mechanisms involved in sense perception. It is now established [2] that a thin layer of gray matter, called the cerebral cortex, is the part of the brain that is concerned with mental processes. Further, this part of the brain can be mapped out into definite areas, each of which is involved in some particular type of consciousness. In the case of sense perception, each such area is connected with the appropriate sense organ by a system of nervous fibers. Impulses received from the external world are conveyed to specific areas of the brain along the afferent nerves which enter the spinal cord at the rear. Thus the reception of sensations, which provide our primary contact with the external world and the original material of thought, is entirely dependent on the healthy condition and efficient functioning of this physiological system.

It is also known that other faculties, like speech, memory, and emotion, are related in a similar way to definite areas of the physical brain. Further, it is now established that, in addition to the mechanics of sensation, speech, memory, and emotion, certain types of *understanding* have the same sort of physical preconditions. The appreciation of the meaning of written words, for example, is dependent on a small part of the cortical layer lying just in front of the visual area. It seems likely that this is true of all processes in the brain, including those involved in abstract thought.

The physiological picture is completed, for our purposes, by a description of the genesis of bodily movements. The muscles controlling movements of the body are connected with the brain by a second set of fibers called efferent nerves; these issue from the spinal cord by ventral roots and carry impulses from the brain to the appropriate muscles. For a bodily movement to occur, it is not even necessary that the brain be involved. In the case of reflex actions, as when the lower part of the leg jumps in response to the tapping of the doctor's little hammer, what happens is that the impulses from the sense organs, conveyed along the afferent nerves, are transferred by a branch across the spinal cord to the efferent nerves, and travel thence to the muscles. A reflex action thus bypasses the brain and is altogether mechanically determined. As a matter of fact, the brain itself is constructed on this same reflex pattern. Exactly the same sort of thing happens when an impulse from the external world takes the longer route through the brain and eventually results in an overt act on the part of the agent. The whole process is of the type of a mechanical reflex action, depending on physical constituents and connections.

It would be true to say, in summary, that everywhere in the brain and nervous system and in human thought and behavior, as described by science, there is a continuous chain of physical, mechanical cause and effect. There are no gaps that must be filled in by postulating an independent soul or mind.

There are good reasons for supposing that the description we have given covers all the *necessary* conditions of man's conscious activities. Injuries to, and operations on, certain specific areas of the brain, affect the corresponding types of consciousness. Particular sensations can be aroused, in the absence of the normal stimuli, by artificially stimulating the appropriate areas of the brain. Patients suffering from brain lesions and epilepsy and people in states of trance or sleepwalking frequently perform complicated actions that have all the appearance of intelligent and purposive direction, although conscious control is in fact altogether absent. The conclusion seems inevitable that the physical mechanisms of the nervous system and brain constitute an unbroken causal chain upon which, to say the least, all the activities that we regard as rational and deliberate are dependent.

On the basis of this evidence alone, it is absurd to regard the body as an inferior, detachable partner in human nature. On the contrary, the physiological nervous system and brain constitute a set of essential material conditions of human consciousness.

A third kind of evidence is provided by physiology in the information it gives us about our *endocrine glands*.[3] The functioning of these glands plays an important part in shaping human temperament and character. The endocrine glands secrete chemical substances called hormones that enter the blood stream and control certain physical changes and emotional reactions. The thyroid gland, situated in the neck, has an important role; if it is underactive, the result is a placid, lethargic type of person; if it is overactive, the temperament is high-strung and excitable. The adrenal gland, near the kidneys, secrets adrenalin. It has several functions. In moments of danger the adrenalin that it adds to the blood increases physical strength and general alertness; when it is overactive it leads to premature sexual development and abnormal muscular strength. The sex glands, in addition to secretions involved in reproduction, control secondary sex characteristics like facial and pubic hair. Generally speaking, the endocrine glands control the fund of available physical, emotional, and mental energy. They provide the material conditions for the formation of temperament and character.

Just as the nervous system and brain furnish the necessary physical conditions of *consciousness,* and the glands the material conditions of *temperament,* so *the physical instincts* play an indispensable role in human *behavior.* The so-called instincts have a rather peculiar status. They are called " *physical,*" but they are obviously not physical in the same sense as the nervous system and glands. You cannot perform a surgical operation and inspect them. They seem to exist on the border line between what is physical in the ordinary sense and what is psychical. They are sometimes called "quasi-biological drives" and, as we shall see, psychology as well as physiology is interested in them. The reasons for postulating the existence of "instincts" are quite clear on the animal level. It is obvious that some animal species possess inborn and unlearned urges to perform complicated series of actions:

"Take the case of the species of wasp known as the solitary wasp. It hatches out from a chrysalis and thus never sees its parents. Yet, it recognizes a certain kind of caterpillar as the right food for its own grub. It stings the caterpillar on a certain nerve center, which has the effect of paralyzing it without killing it, and thus secures that the meat will remain fresh without having to be canned. The wasp then seals the carcass in the nest with the egg. The grub hatches and, behold, its meals are all ready for consumption without the necessity of a tin opener." [4]

The same kind of inborn and unlearned control of behavior is observable all through the animal kingdom, becoming more flexible, and allowing of greater variation of reaction, as we ascend the animal scale. In accordance with the fact of evolution, we should expect to find the same thing in the human species; and of course we do. Everyone is familiar nowadays with the instincts of self-preservation, gregariousness, aggression, sex, and so on. Our behavior, more often than we like to think, is the result, not so much of the rational decision and free choice of an independent soul, as of the innate and often unconscious instinctual drives that appear to be built into our physical nature.

Finally, in this list of physical factors influencing our consciousness, character, and behavior, we must mention *heredity*.[5] The human individual begins as a single fertilized cell in his mother's body. As the cell grows, its nucleus splits up into eel-like threads called chromosomes. The chromosomes are the principal bearers of heredity. Each chromosome is thought to consist of a number of tiny particles known as genes, and each gene is the carrier of a single feature of heredity. The individual receives twenty-four chromosomes from his mother and twenty-four from his father. It is in this way that we receive from our forebears a particular type of physiological equipment. A nervous, glandular, and instinctual apparatus, already disposed in certain definite, if potential, ways, is imposed on us at our conception. And this equipment, about which we have no say or choice, conditions to a very large extent our consciousness, our character, and our behavior. Many of the features and qualities traditionally assigned to the credit of the independent soul are thus inherited through a strictly physiological process. The soul certainly cannot be thought of as inserted into the physical embryo at a certain point in its development. Indeed, it cannot be regarded as a separate entity at all.

This brief and oversimplified account of the part that is played in human life by the purely physical factors in the individual's constitution is almost enough by itself to refute the dualism and libertarianism of the "religious" anthropology. There is a most intimate relationship between the physical constituents of our nature and our mental, volitional, and temperamental aspects. To say the least, these undoubted facts about evolution, the nervous system, the endocrine glands, the physical instincts, and heredity cast some doubt on the view that man has a separate soul or mind capable of thinking and acting and developing character in complete independence of the material basis of human life. This would seem to carry with it the rejection of the notion that man has a spiritual part that is detachable at death, as well as the abandonment of the libertarian interpretation of freedom as unconditioned choice.

The Social Sciences

A second main set of material factors conditioning human life, including functions and activities formerly attributed to the independent soul, may be called the sociological factors. It is not only our inherited physiological equipment, but also our environment, that helps to make us what we are. Part of the environment is, of course, physical in the strict sense; geography, climate, density of population, and so on, all play their part in shaping human physique, temperament, and behavior. But more important than any of these is the social environment. For our society is apt to be the chief source of our values. Our ideas of right and wrong, good and bad, beautiful and ugly, true and false, our notions of what we ought to pursue and avoid — in a word, the ends we aim at in life — are apt to be taken over, more or less uncritically, from the society in which we live. These socially conditioned values, of course, play a part in guiding our behavior and in shaping our habits and characters. Thus our way of life, which we like to think we have chosen freely and rationally, is actually to a considerable extent imposed upon us by social forces. This is another blow against the notion of the free and independent soul.

Anthropology, using the term in the narrower sense in which it denotes one of the social sciences, provides a good deal of the evidence for this estimate of the influence exerted by the social environment. Anthropologists occupy themselves, for the most part, with the study of primitive people. The advantages of this kind of study are that the social unit is small and that the investigator is less apt to be prejudiced in his conclusions by the presuppositions of his own society. Social scientists like Franz Boas, Margaret Mead, and Ruth Benedict have collected an impressive amount of data that seem to prove both the great variety of moral standards that obtain among different peoples and also the extent to which the members of a given society are products of the existing cultural pattern.

Ruth Benedict says:

"The fact of first-rate importance is the predominant role that custom plays in experience and belief, and the great varieties it may manifest. No man ever sees the world with pristine eyes. He sees it edited by a definite set of customs and institutions and ways of thinking. Even in his philosophical probings he cannot go beyond these

stereotypes; his very concepts of the true and the false will still have
reference to his particular traditional customs . . . The life history
of the individual is first ard foremost an accommodation to the patterns and standards traditionally handed down in his community.
From the moment of his birth, the customs into which he is born
shape his experience and behavior. By the time he can talk he is the
little creature of his culture." [6]

A little later on she adds:

"The conditioned response is as automatic as the organically determined, and culturally conditioned responses make up the greater
part of our huge equipment of automatic behavior." [7]

These statements are typical of the kind of conclusions that
anthropologists arrive at on the basis of the evidence that they
have collected. There is general agreement among them that
man is very largely shaped and molded, not only by his inherited
physiological equipment, but also by the norms and conventions
of his society. What the individual thinks and believes, what he
regards as good and bad, the ends he pursues and the way he
behaves, are all conditioned by the "cultural configuration" [8]
in which he lives. His accepted pattern of values and his way of
looking at life are provided by his society.

Disagreement arises when attempts are made to explain the
great variety of cultural patterns and sets of standards that prevail among different peoples. Some are inclined to account for it
by reference to differences in the physical environment, others in
terms of biological differences seated in the chromosomes of the
various races. This is to reduce the second main set of material
factors, the sociological, to the first, the physiological. Ruth Benedict explains the variety in terms of the transmission of different
traditions and historical continuity.

Marx and Engels, a hundred years ago, in one of the earliest
systematic sociological theories of man, explained the variations
in cultural value-patterns as arising out of differences in the underlying economic systems. According to this theory, it is not the

chromosomes of a race or the transmission of a tradition but rather the mode of economic production, exchange, and distribution that is " the real basis, starting from which we can alone work out the ultimate explanation of the whole superstructure of juridical and political institutions as well as of the religious, philosophical, and other ideas of a given historical period." [9] " What individuals are," said Marx, " depends upon the material conditions of their production." [10] Lenin expressed it in this way: " The social understanding of man (that is, his various views and teaching, philosophical, religious, political, etc.) reflect the economic structure of society." [11] Finally, Marx put the theory in a nutshell: " The human essence . . . in its reality is the ensemble of the social relations." [12] In this view, the characteristics, values, and beliefs of a society are determined by, and therefore reflect the nature of, the economic forces that are at work.

This Marxist theory of economic determinism is just one attempt to explain why one society selects a certain set of values and another society a different set. But it assumes the truth of the now widespread sociological view that norms and ends are relative to social forces and that the individuals in a society take over their values, more or less uncritically and unconsciously, from their society, of which they are therefore themselves largely automatic products and reflections.

Another important question is this: How does it happen that these different cultural value-patterns, which are in fact entirely relative and conventional, are regularly assumed by their adherents to enjoy absolute and eternal status? Ruth Benedict connects it with the universal tendency to differentiate sharply between the " in-group " and the " out-group." The members of the " in-group " regard themselves as alone really human and their norms as therefore alone truly valid. Marxism develops a typical variation on this theme. In the Marxist view, as we have seen, the cultural pattern reflects the existing economic conditions. The ruling classes, who benefit most from the economic arrangements, want them to remain the same forever and to be regarded as final and unchangeable. They set about fulfilling this desire obliquely by persuading the whole society that the existing values and beliefs, which reflect the economy, have an absolute status and enjoy divine sanction.

In any case, it is agreed by both Benedict and the Marxists that it is man's incurable self-interest and self-conceit that exalt his relative and earthly values to high and heavenly places. We shall subsequently examine both the psychological [13] and the Biblical [14] versions of this doctrine. But the main point seems well-established: the prevailing customs, norms, and beliefs are not only accepted uncritically by the majority in a society, so that their typical actions and thoughts are socially conditioned, but are also regarded as having absolute validity and divine sanction. Hence the members of the society come to have a highly developed sense of obligation towards these norms and a shattering sense of guilt when they contravene them; at the same time, those who refuse to follow the currently accepted way of life are reviled as evildoers, sinners, and rebels against God. The repressive, authoritarian morality, familiar to us as part of the " religious " anthropology, has this sociological derivation.

The upshot of this discussion is that we have to add to the weight of strictly physical factors in making us what we are this second set of material factors, the sociological. It becomes increasingly impossible to think of the individual's character, in all its facets, as created by the free, rational choices of his independent soul. It is beginning to look more as if he is the product of the combination of his inherited physiological apparatus and an externally imposed cultural pattern. At the very least, it is certain that material factors, both physical and social, furnish the inescapable conditions of the individual's development. The truth of body-soul dualism must be denied, and the validity of the repressive, authoritarian morality begins to be called in question.

PSYCHOLOGY

A third set of material factors that are operative in making man what he is, in conditioning his character, his thought, and his behavior, is exposed by modern psychological investigation. The greatest name in this field is Sigmund Freud, who, in spite of many subsequent modifications of his theories, set the general tone and direction of this science.

We might well begin by asking in what sense the psyche can be said to be the source of further material determinants in human life. Have we not at last arrived at the soul? The answer is that the psyche investigated by psychology is by no means to be confused with the soul or mind as understood in the old body-soul dualism. In fact " the psyche " is a kind of abstraction from the organism as a whole; those aspects of the organism for which the term " psyche " stands cannot be separated from the rest of the organism, except artificially and for purposes of analysis. First of all, in the Freudian scheme, the essence of the psyche is constituted by what we have previously called the instincts, and these innate " drives," as Freud calls them, are commonly known as " physical," or, at any rate, " quasi-biological." Secondly, conscious or mental life, which is certainly an activity of the psyche is, as we have seen, intimately related to the physiological nervous system and brain. " We assume," wrote Freud, " that mental life is the function of an apparatus to which we ascribe the character of being extended in space." [15] This physiological apparatus, however, according to Freud, is vitalized or energized by instinctual drives and, in this capacity, is called the " id." Freud recognized, of course, that these drives, like the whole of the psychical life, are closely associated with the body: they " originate in the somatic organization." [16]

The id and its instincts are unconscious in their activities. Consciousness, or what we commonly call the mind or reason and what Freud called the ego, is said to be a " modification of the id " due to the sense organs. Reason is that part of the id which is modified by the external world through the medium of the sense organs. Since the ego is actually a part of the id, our conscious activities are apt to be determined as much, if not more, by the unconscious drives of the id as by the information given by the senses.

According to Freud, there is a second modification of the id that is induced by the pressures of society. The basic instinctual drives are the life or sex instincts and the death or aggressive instincts. These begin to express themselves and to seek satisfaction in infancy but immediately encounter opposition from parents and nurses. The latter are the representatives of society and the mediators of the taboos and prohibitions that society imposes on the dangerous and anarchical instincts. The result of this encounter between the pleasure-seeking instincts and the restricting moral rules of society, mediated by the parents with their greatly superior strength, is that the infant's instincts are repressed into the unconscious. There they do not cease to function but live on and continue to seek satisfaction. They must do so now, however, " in disguise " and " along circuitous routes." Eventually, the child comes to terms with his parents and his society by taking the taboos and prohibitions into himself in the form of " conscience." Thus a further modification of the id is produced, which Freud called the " superego " and which now imposes moral rules on the ego.

This is the normal process by which the notorious Oedipus complex is resolved. The Oedipus complex is itself a regular feature in the growth of the individual. The infant finds in his mother the first object of his sex instinct, and in his father, the rival for his mother's affection, the first object of his aggressive instinct. To put it vividly, he desires sexual intercourse with his mother and wants to kill his father. This is obviously an intolerable situation since the infant is physically unable to fulfill either of these wishes. The unhappy state of affairs is overcome when the child finds a love object other than his mother and when he identifies himself with his father. When he identifies himself with his father, the representative of the social prohibitions, he absorbs these taboos into his own psyche in the form of a moral conscience or superego. At the same time, he projects an ideal father-image into the heavens and calls it his Heavenly Father. This Heavenly Father now takes over the functions formerly discharged by the male parent; he becomes the source of protection and security, the purveyor and guarantor of the moral laws, the omniscient and omnipotent creator, judge, and ruler. The moral laws are thus hedged about by supernatural sanctions and backed by threats and promises that have to do with the future life.

The taboos and prohibitions of morality, reinforced by the sanctions of religion, are imposed on the ego by the superego with " ruthless severity." Freud attempted to explain the authoritarian character of the moral conscience by suggesting, first, that the superego wins as its ally all the energy of the aggressive instinct which is now directed against the ego, and, secondly, that the degree of severity with which the superego imposes its demands is proportionate to the difficulty encountered in overcoming the Oedipus complex.

This is the psychoanalytical account of the genesis of repressive and authoritarian morality. The content of this ethics is the code of rules by which society seeks to curb the dangerous natural instincts. Its severity is due to the psychical mechanisms involved in resolving the Oedipus complex. Finally, Freud and countless psychiatrists since have discovered that this kind of morality and " religion " are a fruitful source of neuroses, the psychical ailments that distort the outlook and destroy the happiness of so many millions of people.

The religious and moral beliefs that the individual thinks he adopts because of their objective truth and justice are thus explained in terms of a collision between the physical instincts and the restraints of society. In the same way, Freud went on to show how philosophical theories, character traits, peculiarities of speech, behavior, and dress, and even choice of profession — in fact, everything that goes to make up the individual's character and personality — can be explained by the psychoanalytical theory of man. Even if this is only part of the truth, it is obvious that we tend greatly to overestimate the power of reason and the role of free choice in human life. Reason, said Freud, is the " poor crea-ture " and the " slave " [17] of the id and the superego. It is like the rider of a powerful horse who, in the last analysis, has to go where the horse wants to go.[18] And if reason turns to the external world, it simply finds there a third master in the shape of the " neces-sity " that rules everywhere in nature.[19]

It is clear enough that the investigations of the psyche lead to the same conclusions as the researches of the physiological and sociological sciences. First, the sciences of man indicate that the relationship between the physical and psychical is such that the old body-soul dualism has to be unequivocally rejected. Secondly, the enormous part that is played in shaping human character by physiological conditions, by sociological forces, by unconscious instinctual drives, and by all kinds of psychical mechanisms com-pletely refutes the libertarian conception of freedom. Finally, the origin and genesis of rigoristic morality, as well as its terrible psychological dangers, are exposed for all to see.

In short, the findings of the modern sciences, physical, social, and psychological, constitute the strongest possible refutation of the " religious " anthropology, with its dualistic analysis of man, its repressive and authoritarian version of ethics, and its libertar-ian interpretation of freedom. At the same time, if it is true that the Biblical view of man is quite different from the " religious," this scientific evidence does not necessarily weaken the Biblical position.[20] The conflict here is between science and " religion," and not between science and Christianity, at any rate in so far as the Christian view remains free of " religious " infection.

CHAPTER VI

Scientific Naturalism

IF THE SCIENTIFIC EVIDENCE once and for all refutes the doctrines of the " religious " anthropology, the same evidence can easily lead to a set of opposite errors. These errors constitute what we may call the " scientific " anthropology.[1] It is sometimes also referred to as the " naturalistic " view of man. We can understand and sympathize with this position both as a reaction against the excesses of the " religious " anthropology and also as a not unnatural elaboration of the scientific evidence. At the same time there are many cogent reasons for insisting that it fails to do justice to the heights and depths of human nature.

Each doctrine of the " scientific " anthropology stands at the opposite extreme to some doctrine of the " religious " anthropology. Thus, in opposition to body-soul dualism, we find here an oversimplified, one-level materialism that denies the reality, in any sense, of the human spirit. This denial carries with it, of course, the assertion of the finality of death over against the doctrine of the immortality of the soul. In the next place, as against the libertarian conception of freedom, the " scientific " anthropology embraces an absolute determinism. And finally, by way of an easily understandable, if extreme, reaction against the authoritarian, repressive morality, we encounter a complete relativism, frequently combined with a self-expression psychology.

The Denial of Spirit

The oversimplified, one-level materialism of the " scientific " anthropology holds that man is nothing but a complicated animal, who can be exhaustively explained in terms appropriate to the explanation of the animal kingdom. In most cases the animal in turn is regarded as simply a bundle of animated matter completely explicable in the quantitative and mechanical categories of classical or Newtonian physics. The concepts which, in the nineteenth century at any rate, seemed sufficient for the description of nonhuman nature are held to be equally adequate for the description of the human being.

One aspect of man's being that appears to differentiate him from the rest of nature is his capacity for rational reflection or thought. How is it possible to explain this faculty in terms of the naturalistic hypothesis? In answering this question, we must first of all remind ourselves of the physiological facts that we have previously noted. The reflex mechanisms that constitute the nervous system and brain appear to be sufficient to account for the whole of human behavior. There appears to be no need for the postulate of conscious thought or decision. The theory that it is unnecessary to introduce the concept of conscious mind at all in order to explain the behavior of man is the most straightforward form of materialism. It is usually known as "behaviorism."

According to behaviorism, when we say that "man has a mind" or possesses the faculty of thought or is an intelligent being, we simply mean that he is a kind of animal that tends to behave in certain ways under certain conditions. The only evidence available to A that might lead him to conclude that B "has a mind" is the fact that B tends to behave in certain ways in response to certain tests that A applies. According to this theory it follows that "having a mind" or "possessing the faculty of thought" *means* "tending to behave in certain ways in certain situations." And these various ways of behaving, though often extremely complicated, are nonetheless entirely explicable in terms of the reflex mechanisms of the physiological nervous system and brain. In short, all types of so-called "mental" activity are reducible to physical and mechanical behavior. When I say that A "has a good mind," I mean that he tends to respond in a spec-

ifiable manner to specifiable tests. When I say that I am thinking, I mean that certain movements are occurring in my larynx,
throat, and tongue. When I say that I feel nervous, I mean that
certain changes are taking place in my blood pressure. When I
say that I see a red patch, I mean that certain activities are going
on in my nervous system and brain.

There are a great many reasons for rejecting this most unambiguous form of materialism. Perhaps the most decisive was
pointed out by C. D. Broad. It may be true, he said, that whenever I have a sensation, a movement takes place in my brain, but
it should be obvious to anyone that the sensation is not reducible
to the movement. For one thing, certain questions may be quite
properly asked about the physiological event that would be nonsense if referred to the sensation, and vice versa; we may ask of
the movement whether it be swift or slow, straight or crooked,
but none of these adjectives make sense if applied to the sensation; conversely we may ask of the state of awareness whether
it is clear or confused while such a question becomes absurd in
relation to the movement in the brain.[2] Moreover, it would be
theoretically possible for a surgeon to open my skull at the moment of my awareness of a red patch and to inspect my brain; he
could then observe the physiological movements but obviously he
would catch no glimpse of my state of awareness.

Considerations of this kind tell heavily against the behavioristic explanation. It is therefore more usual to encounter the
weaker form of materialism known as " epiphenomenalism." In
this view, thought or consciousness is regarded as an accompani-
ment or function or product of the physiological processes of the
body. Each event in consciousness is correlated with a physiological event that it accompanies or immediately succeeds. This corre-
lation is usually held to be a causal relation, such that the physiological events are the causes of the conscious events. Moreover,
according to this theory, there are no causal relations between the
events of consciousness but only between physiological events, the

sequence of physiological events being reflected in the sequence of mental events. Thus the events of consciousness are like the shadows cast by the moving parts of a machine or the noises of turning wheels or the smells that issue from a factory. This is the force of the term " epiphenomena " as applied to mental activities.

In so far as epiphenomenalism at least recognizes the fact of consciousness and holds it to be in some sense distinct from the physiological factors on which it is dependent, it is a milder form of materialism than the behaviorist theory. But it also has its crude version. An example is the well-known remark, attributed to the nineteenth century physiologist Cabanis, that " the brain secretes thought as the liver secretes bile." In this crude form of epiphenomenalism, man is nothing but a bundle of physico-chemical substances the behavior of which is entirely determined by the mechanical laws of motion. Thought is the phosphorescence surrounding the bundle. Love is a chemical commotion. Human conduct is the automatic product of conditioned reflexes. In short, man is reduced altogether to the physical level and is completely immersed in nature. There is little to choose between this form of materialism and the behavioristic theory.

A more subtle and therefore more formidable type of epiphenomenalism is found in the Marxist anthropology. The favorite Marxist way of describing the allegedly epiphenomenal relationship between mind and matter is to say that the former is a *reflection* of the latter. Marx himself, in contrasting his view with Hegel's, wrote: " With me, on the contrary, the ideal [thought] is nothing else than the material world reflected by the human mind and translated into forms of thought." [3] According to Lenin, there are " scores of instances where Engels speaks of things and their reflections in the human brain, in our consciousness, thought, etc. Engels does not say that sensations or ideas are ' symbols ' of things, for consistent materialism must here use ' image,' ' picture,' or ' reflection,' instead of ' symbol.' " [4] Lenin specifically distinguished Engels' view from that of Cabanis:

" Engels dissociated himself from the 'vulgar' materialists . . . they erred in believing that the brain secretes thought in the same way as the liver secretes bile." [5] Lenin also insisted that the Marxist position was different from the crude materialism of Hobbes and, by implication, the behaviorists, who *identify* thought with some kind of physical activity: " To say that thought is material is to take a false step, a step toward confusing materialism and idealism . . . that the conception of 'matter' must also include 'thought' . . . is a muddle, for if such an inclusion is made, the epistemological contrast between mind and matter loses all meaning." [6] He went on, of course, to warn that " the epistemological contrast between mind and matter " must not be turned into a metaphysical opposition. The point that he was anxious to establish was that human consciousness, on the Marxist theory, is not to be *identified with,* but is a *reflection of,* matter. Or, as he put it elsewhere in a significant phrase to which we shall return, consciousness is " one of the properties of matter in motion " [7]; " it is the transformation of the energy of external excitation into a state of consciousness." [8]

Thus, for epiphenomenalism, thought is to be distinguished from physical activity, to which it is nonetheless tied as a copy is tied to the original. Moreover, the greatest possible stress is placed on the alleged primacy of matter over mind. " Materialism," said Lenin, " in full agreement with the natural sciences, takes matter as primary and regards consciousness, thought, and sensation as secondary." [9] There are two main arguments advanced in this connection. First, it is pointed out that matter comes first chronologically; mind is a late development in the evolutionary process. According to Engels, " mind itself is merely the highest product of matter." [10] Consciousness is an evolutionary development of some potentiality that is present in matter from the beginning. " In the foundation of the structure of matter," said Lenin, " we can only surmise the existence of a faculty akin to sensation." [11] When matter, at a late stage in its evolution,

becomes "organized in a definite way," [12] it produces consciousness as one of its "properties." This is taken to prove that matter is prior, in every sense, to mind.

The second argument that the Marxists use to prove that mind
is secondary to matter is the fact that consciousness, as far as we
know, occurs only in association with a physical brain. *"It is impossible,"* according to Marx, *"to separate thought from matter
that thinks."* [13] Engels put it this way: "Our consciousness and
thinking, however supersensuous they may be, are the product
of a material bodily organ, the brain." [14] In our experience,
thought cannot take place apart from a physical brain. This fact,
again, is held by Marxists to establish the priority of matter over
mind.

For Marxism, then, thought is altogether dependent on matter.
Thinking is simply a reflection of the motions of matter. The only
arguments, however, that are employed to support this theory are,
first, the chronological priority of matter, and, second, the fact that
the presence of a physical brain appears to be a necessary condition for the occurrence of thought.

A somewhat similar epiphenomenalist point of view is suggested by the few remarks that Sigmund Freud made on this
subject. The ego or conscious mind is, he said, merely "a modification of the id." The id is the most fundamental aspect of the
psyche, and the psyche as a whole is regarded as something "extended in space." In other words, the psyche is essentially a physical structure "which gives rise to the phenomena of consciousness only at a particular point and under certain conditions." [15]
In so far as the psyche is something "extended in space," it is
apparently equated with the physiological nervous system and
brain. [16] This structure is, first of all, vitalized by the instincts,
and the instincts themselves are said to "originate in the somatic
[i.e., bodily] organization," [17] and of course they constitute the
essential elements of the id. In the next place, this same structure, "under certain conditions," gives rise to consciousness.

" From what was originally a cortical layer, provided with organs for receiving stimuli, . . . a special organization has arisen intermediary between the id and the external world. This region of our mental life has been given the name of ego." [18]

This is very similar to Lenin's statement that consciousness is a product or property of " matter organized in a definite way." And just as in Marxism thought is a " reflection " of, and is therefore tied and bound to, matter, so in Freud the ego is a " modification " of the id, to which it tends to be related as a slave to its master. The ego is " like a man on horseback who has to hold in check the superior strength of the horse . . . [and] often is obliged to guide it where it wants to go." [19]

Ultimately, then, for Freud as for Marx, the " somatic organization " is primary and consciousness secondary. But this is epiphenomenalism and not the crude materialism of Hobbes and the behaviorists. For a clear distinction is drawn between consciousness and the matter of which it is a product. Freud even suggested that there is something mysterious and scientifically inexplicable in human consciousness. Our acts of consciousness, he wrote,[20] are " immediate data and cannot be more fully explained." At the same time, his identification of the psyche with something "extended in space," as well as his low estimate of reason as the " poor creature " and " submissive slave " [21] of the id, make it clear that Freud attempted to explain the human mind in entirely materialistic terms.

Epiphenomenalism in general wants to reduce the human spirit to an inferior role and to make it a mere shadow of the physical reality of which it is a product. The first step in this reduction is a disparagement of human reason in which matter is given an absolute priority over mind. This aspect of the " scientific " anthropology is a complete reversal of the virtual deification of reason, accompanied by a disparagement of the body, in the " religious " anthropology.

The Denial of Freedom and Values

A second stage in the attack on the reality and importance of the human spirit takes the form of the denial of human freedom. Absolute determinism is a regular feature of the "scientific" anthropology. And it is easy enough to see how this conclusion is reached both as a reaction to the excessive claims of the libertarian conception of freedom and also under the weight of the scientific evidence. As we have seen, there are three sets of material factors that play a tremendously powerful role in conditioning our behavior, our beliefs, our values, and our whole way of life. In the face of the kind of evidence provided by the physiological, sociological, and psychological sciences, it is natural indeed to conclude that man is nothing but a more or less automatic product of these various material forces. The conclusion is all the more inevitable if we have already decided that human consciousness is nothing but a function of physiological processes.

The best known and most influential types of absolute determinism are, again, found in behaviorism, Marxism, and Freudianism. These theories spring respectively from interest in physiology, sociology, and psychology. And it is significant that each theory selects, as the all-determining factor in human life, just that particular set of material factors which it is concerned to study. Thus, for behaviorism man's behavior is nothing but the product of mechanical, conditioned reflexes. For Marxism man is nothing but "the ensemble of the social relations" [22] and is determined entirely by economic forces. And for Freud the human being is nothing but a set of "psychical mechanisms" formed as a result of the collision between the natural instincts and the restraints of society.

In all probability, most contemporary determinists would agree that each of these theories is one-sided in its preoccupation with one set of material factors. At the same time, they would answer this obvious objection, and also strengthen the determinist case, by combining the three theories and by arguing that man is a product of all three sets of material forces.

Freud himself came close to doing just that, and we may take his views as representative of the determinist position. He did not scruple to label his theory, " absolute psychical determinism." [23] As we have seen, the ego or reason is, first of all, the submissive slave of the id, and the id consists primarily of natural instincts, operating blindly and inexorably. But the ego is also, secondly, the more or less helpless servant of what Freud called the " superego " or moral conscience. And this moral conscience is a social product, its content consisting of taboos and prohibitions, derived from society, internalized in the psyche during the resolution of the Oedipus complex, and imposed on the ego with " ruthless severity " by the superego. If the poor ego attempts to free itself from these two masters, the id and the superego, by turning to the external world, it simply encounters there a third master in the form of the absolute " necessity " that rules everywhere in nature. Thus the ego is " a poor creature, owing service to three masters and consequently menaced by three several dangers: from the external world, from the libido of the id, and from the severity of the superego." [24] In other words, the individual is the more or less helpless product of physical, psychological, and sociological forces.

Freud thus recognized the three sets of material factors: the physical environment to which we have access through our sense organs and ego, our physiological equipment, including the instincts which constitute the id, and the social environment which is the source of the taboos of the superego. The thought, behavior, and character of the individual are simply the precipitate of the interaction of these three great forces. Our most cherished beliefs about life and reality, our deepest convictions about good and evil, our noble and ignoble actions, our ingrained traits and our most casual mannerisms, and indeed everything that we are and would like to be are simply the automatic product of the psychical mechanisms that nature and society have combined to manufacture in us.

Thus everything that the "religious" anthropology had ascribed to the free and independent soul is here attributed to the blind operation of strictly material forces. Indeed, if the human spirit, in all its ramifications, is a mere shadow of its physical basis, we might have expected that man's freedom would turn out to be an illusion.

A third conclusion to which the scientific evidence is very apt to lead is that of complete relativism. Anthropologists have discovered not only that the members of a given society are very largely conditioned in their value-judgments by the traditional mores, ends, and ways of looking at things that are characteristic of their culture, but also that there is a very wide variety of cultural patterns as between different societies. It is very tempting to conclude that *all* values are *entirely* relative to a given society. On this view, all norms and principles are, in fact, mere social conventions and vary from one society to another. There are no objective, universal values and standards that belong to the nature of things.

We are likely to be attracted by this theory of value not only by the evidence as to the great variety of norms adopted by different societies at different times, but also by the fact that each society tends to take it for granted that its values are absolute and eternal. This latter claim is so very obviously false that we are apt to react at once in the opposite direction and to conclude that there are no absolute values at all. We have then arrived, whether we like it or not, at complete relativism.

If we were to inquire whether it is not significant that all men appear, on the evidence, to yearn after and to pursue some absolutes in the realm of values, the "scientific" anthropology has various answers at its disposal. Ruth Benedict relates the production of absolutes to man's deep-rooted tendency to draw a sharp line between the "in-group" and the "out-group." Along with this division there goes the conviction that the members of the " in-group " are alone fully human, and that, therefore, their values alone are really valid. Marx attributed the absolutizing of relative values to the fact that the latter are projections and rationalizations of the existing economic system; the ruling classes who benefit from the economic *status quo* and, therefore, want it to be regarded as absolute and unchangeable, are successful in foisting upon the whole society the notion that the corresponding values are eternal and divinely sanctioned. Freud associates this human tendency with the resolution of the Oedipus complex; the conventional norms of society, previously mediated by the male parent with his absolute authority, are, at this stage in the psyche's development, internalized and, being regarded as the voice of God, who is a " father-image " projected into the heavens, are considered to be absolute and eternal.

As for the moral obligation that is felt toward these values and the sense of sin that is experienced when they are violated, Freud offered the most plausible naturalistic explanation. The superego or conscience imposes its laws on the psyche with " ruthless severity," partly because it is the representative of the authoritarian male parent and partly because it commandeers for its own purposes all the power of the aggressive instinct. The result is that the natural instincts are thwarted in their natural expression and are compelled to seek gratification in unnatural and often neurotic ways. Moral obligation and the sense of sin are simply elements in this unnatural and neurotic human situation.

The final outcome of this line of thought now appears almost inevitably. All moral rules are really just relative social taboos mistaken for divine commandments. The sense of obligation, guilt, and sin arises as part of this mistake and has disastrous psychological consequences. In order to overcome this unhealthy condition, we must first of all get rid of the sense of obligation and of sin. We can do this if we understand that these feelings are more or less neurotic and come into being as a result of mistaking relative social conventions for absolute laws. It is easy enough at this point to conclude that morality as such is neurotic, to recommend that all taboos, prohibitions, and even the distinction between right and wrong itself be rejected, and to suggest that the way to the good life is to permit the natural instincts and impulses to gratify themselves without let or hindrance of any kind. Thus we arrive at the position of " free self-expression."

This conclusion, of course, constitutes a complete reversal of the repressive, authoritarian moralism. Rigoristic moralism not only believes that there are absolute standards but supposes that it knows what they are in detail. The self-expression school of thought insists that all standards are completely relative and are devices of society for suppressing the natural instincts. Moralism believes that in obedience to the absolute moral laws it is necessary to combat the physical instincts by rigorous, authoritarian control, and that this leads to the good life. The self-expression theory insists that in fact this kind of moralistic authoritarianism results in psychological ruin and recommends, on the contrary, the uninhibited gratification of the instincts and impulses. Moralism believes that its ethical code is the will of God for man. The exponents of self-expression, equating all ethics with moralism, condemn morality in general as the worst disease of the human lot.

CRITICISM

The chief weakness of the " scientific " anthropology is a failure to recognize that the scientific evidence is not the only available evidence about the nature of man. This failure in turn is based on the primary dogma of scientism, which holds that empirical science is the sole source of genuine knowledge and that the scientific method is the only valid way to truth. Thus, instead of simply claiming that the scientific evidence is *part* of the evidence about man's nature and that the scientific method is *one* of the ways to truth, the " scientific " anthropology claims that the various sciences give the *whole* truth about the human condition.

As a result of this characteristic pretension, scientism, instead of saying that man is in many respects an animal, says that he is *nothing but* an animal; instead of saying that human consciousness is genetically a property of matter organized in a certain way, it says that thought is *nothing but* an epiphenomenon of matter; instead of saying that man is largely conditioned by irrational material forces, it says that he is *nothing but* a product of such factors; instead of saying that current values are very often only the relative conventions of a particular society, it says that values *as such* are *nothing but* conventions of this kind; and, finally, instead of noting that morality is frequently confused with repressive moralism and, in that case, leads to neuroses, it identifies morality *as such* with puritanism, and advocates its abolition.

In comparing the scientific evidence with the " scientific " anthropology, it is easy enough to overlook the transition from " in many respects " and " very often " to " nothing but " and " as such." If we do this, we shall be strongly impressed by the plausibility of the " scientific " account of man. And indeed, as long as the " scientific " anthropology sticks to the scientific facts, it occupies an unshakable position. For this reason, there is, as we shall see, a very large degree of truth in its contentions. But as soon as the " scientific " anthropology substitutes " nothing but " for " in many respects " it ceases to be science and becomes scientism. It is just this substitution that constitutes the difference, small enough to all appearances but vast in its implications, between what is scientific and what is " scientific," between science and scientism.

With these general considerations in mind, we shall now go on to examine in more detail the various doctrines of the " scientific " anthropology. First of all, there is the epiphenomenalist account of human consciousness and thought. We shall concentrate on Marxism as one of the clearest versions of this theory.

It is not relevant to our purposes to explain the many objections to the naïve representationalism of the Marxist theory of perception. But it is pertinent to ask what the Marxists mean when they describe thought as a *reflection* of matter. What is the nature of this reflection? What is its ontological status? Lenin insisted that it is *not* material in nature. Thus to confuse mind and matter, after the fashion of Hobbes and the behaviorists, is, he said, a " muddle " and a " false step "; it is to make idealism and materialism indistinguishable. But if consciousness is not material in nature, in what sense does this deserve to be called a materialistic explanation of mind? In actual fact, the nature of consciousness, admittedly different from the nature of matter, remains as much a mystery as it is in the dualistic theory. In fact, we do not seem to have escaped at all from dualism. Gilbert Ryle's description of dualism as the " ghost in the machine " theory [25] is even more apt when applied to epiphenomenalism; for on this theory consciousness is indeed a kind of ghostly and inexplicable counterpart of physiological processes.

The only attempt that the Marxist version of epiphenomenalism makes to justify its claim to give a materialistic account of consciousness is to point to two well-known facts: first, mind is an evolutionary development out of matter, and, second, thought appears to require as a necessary condition the presence of a physical brain and nervous system. After mentioning these two facts, Engels immediately asserts that " this is, of course, pure materialism." [26]

In regard to the first of these facts, we may point out that if its recognition were tantamount to the adoption of pure materialism, then almost all modern theologians would have to be called pure materialists. The late Archbishop William Temple, for instance, made a great deal of this fact on which he based a very different theory. He agreed with Lenin that since nature produces mind, something akin to mind must be present all through the process; but he concluded from this that since mind alone contains an ultimate principle of explanation, namely, explanation in terms of purpose, it follows that mind and not matter provides the key to the meaning of the whole.[27]

In any case, to suppose that the emergence of mind out of matter somehow reduces mind to the same level as matter (and surely something like this must be meant by the Marxist insistence that its account is materialistic) is to make two mistakes. First, it amounts to a refusal to take evolution *seriously;* it is a failure to recognize that evolution is a process of genuine *development,* in which characteristics and faculties that are really *new* emerge. Secondly, it stumbles into the well-known genetic or reductionist fallacy; this is the fallacy of supposing that when you have traced the development of X back to its ultimate origins, you have reduced X to the level of these primitive beginnings; it is the mistake of describing the end product of a long line of development as " nothing but " a form of its earliest stages, as though, for example, modern medicine could be adequately defined as really only a form of the witchcraft of the primitive medicine man.

Underlying these two mistakes is the assumption that explanation of the later in terms of the earlier is always to be preferred to explanation of the earlier in terms of the later. The former or naturalistic type of explanation is, of course, more suited to the purposes of science; it is for this reason that scientism or the " scientific " anthropology regards it as alone valid. The latter kind of explanation, often called teleological, was favored by traditional metaphysics and is therefore suspect in a " scientific " age. Actually it is impossible to prove that either type of explanation has any innate superiority over the other or any exclusive claim to truth and ultimate validity. Temple, using the teleological approach in interpreting nature and evolution, arrived, on the basis of exactly the same evidence, at a conclusion very different from the Marxists, who use the naturalistic method. Clearly, both the naturalistic and the teleological types of explanation have their place, and it is a misuse of words to say that one is the more

" true " than the other. To assume the sole validity of explanation in terms of prior material causes is the mark of scientism.

As for the second "argument," which has to do with the fact that the presence of a physical brain and nervous system is a necessary condition of thought, again there are few in any field who would deny that this is a fact. But this fact has no materialistic implications, in the usual sense. The fact that X is the indispensable condition of the occurrence of Y, and that Y never appears unless X is present, by no means proves that X is prior to Y in terms of reality or of importance. For example, the presence of a physical canvas and of physical pigments is a necessary condition of the occurrence of a pictorial work of art; but it would be absurd to argue that therefore the materials are primary and the picture itself secondary in terms of aesthetic value.

We have to conclude that what the scientific evidence establishes is simply the fact that man is closely related to the animal and that mind is deeply implicated in matter; the intimacy of the relationship in both cases refutes all forms of body-soul dualism. But the evidence by no means proves that the abstraction called " matter " has any kind of priority (except chronological) over the abstraction called " mind."

Passing on to the question of free will *versus* determinism, we have to distinguish again between the scientific evidence, admittedly fatal to the libertarian conception of freedom, and the deterministic doctrine of the " scientific " anthropology. This is a doctrine of *absolute* determinism; it states that man is *nothing but* a helpless product of the material factors to which he is exposed. It is true, of course, that the individual is very often and to a considerable extent a precipitate of such forces. But the theory of absolute determinism has one rather serious defect: it happens to be self-refuting. It is self-refuting in the sense that, if it were true, we should never be in a position to know that it is true. If we were entirely immersed in the mechanical network of natural cause and effect, we should never be aware of that fact — any more than the atoms or the animals are aware of it. The fact that a human being can arrive at a theory of absolute determinism, that is to say, can claim to know that "everything" operates in accordance with the laws that govern natural-cause-and-effect series, proves that the human being, at any rate in the act of knowing, is different from the "everything" that he knows. For if the act of knowing (for instance, knowing that absolute determinism is true) were itself an item in the "everything" that is known (and known to be determined), then this act of knowing would simply be one event in the natural-cause-and-effect series, like the movement of an atom; and if this were the case, then this act of knowing could no more claim to be "true" than the movement of an atom could be described as "true."

Another way of saying the same thing is to point out that absolute determinism entails complete irrationalism, and complete irrationalism is the end of all intelligent discourse and argument. Absolute determinism claims that all thinking is entirely determined by irrational material factors, either physiological, sociological, or psychological, or a combination of all three. But this doctrine is obviously a two-edged sword that cuts both ways. Or, to use another familiar metaphor, he who asserts this doctrine can easily be "hoist with his own petard." For the doctrine is an act of thinking, and if all thinking is determined by irrational factors, then this act of thinking must be similarly determined. It would simply be an event, like other events; and events are neither true nor false; they either happen or they do not happen.

The conclusion to which we are driven is that while, on the basis of the scientific evidence, we have to recognize that determinism holds true of man's nature to a far greater extent than libertarianism understands, nevertheless it cannot be the whole truth about man. There are depths of man's being, apparently related to his special type of consciousness, in regard to which the doctrine of determinism simply does not make sense.

When we come to examine the position of complete relativism

in values, and the accompanying recommendation of free self-expression in conduct, we have to admit again that there is much that is true and valuable in these theories. It is undeniable that many popularly accepted " values " are merely relative social conventions that are turned into absolutes, very often as the results of the operation of various types of egotistic self-affirmation, both in the individual and in the group. Further, this process often results in the psychological disaster of authoritarian moralism, against which self-expression psychology is an understandable reaction. But complete relativism makes the mistake of supposing that because many, even most, so-called values can be shown to be relative and conventional, therefore *all* values are relative and there are *no* universal and eternal norms. Similarly, self-expression psychology confuses moralism with morality as *such* and refuses to admit the possibility of a valid ethics.

There are several reasons for objecting to complete relativism. First of all, let us examine the question of the variety of standards adopted in different societies. We can point out, at once, that it does not logically follow, as many anthropologists seem to assume, that because many of the ideas of right and wrong adopted in one society can be shown to be contradicted in another society, there are therefore *no* universal norms of conduct. As a matter of fact, the extent of the actual variation is usually exaggerated because of a tendency to overlook one very important fact. It is well-known to anthropologists that within any society of people there is always an " in-group," or what we shall call " the basic social unit." And the fact, the significance of which is usually lost on anthropologists, is that moral obligation is regarded as binding *only within this group*. One is bound to do what is right and to avoid what is wrong in one's dealings with members of this basic social unit. One's conduct toward those outside the unit need be governed only by expediency; for these outsiders are not really human and the human moral standards do not apply to them.

If we bear this fact in mind in our study of the mores of different peoples, we shall find that there exists, not an infinite variety of opinion at all, but rather a very general agreement as to what is right and wrong in the relations of members of the basic social unit. There is a remarkable unanimity on the part of all societies at all times that within whatever is regarded as the basic social unit — whether it is the matriarchal line or the tribe or the nation — it is right to tell the truth and wrong to tell lies, right to keep one's word and wrong to violate a pledge, right to be loyal and wrong to be treacherous, right to help and wrong to hinder one another, right to defend one's own social unit and wrong to run away in the face of dangers that threaten it, right to give to every man his due and wrong to cheat, right to be moderate and controlled in the gratification of one's appetites and wrong to be licentious and abandoned. In other words, honesty, honor, loyalty, kindness, courage, justice, and self-control are universally recognized as valid standards, within the basic social unit. No doubt this list could be extended, but this is enough to make the point.

Ruth Benedict, who is a cultural relativist, attempted to clinch the case for complete relativism by citing an obscure tribe in New Guinea who think it right to practice lies, deceit, and treachery toward each other. She happened to mention, however, in passing, that they did not act in this way toward other members of the same matriarchal line.[28] Obviously, in this case, the matriarchal line was the basic social unit; one had to behave morally only toward members of this group; all others were enemies and it was quite permissible to deceive and lie to one's enemies.

Anthropologists are also apt to be deceived by the fact that they are largely preoccupied with the study of primitive peoples. We should expect to find here a considerable diversity of moral standards, since primitive man is obviously more likely than his sophisticated successor to be conditioned by impersonal forces in his behavior. But even here, if we examine the practices that

obtain within the "in-group," we find allegiance to the fundamental norms. If we then proceed to study the higher ethics of
the great civilizations from the Egyptian and Chinese to our own,
we find a unanimity so unmistakable that even an anthropologist
could not miss it. The ethics of Confucius, Buddha, Zoroaster,
and Jesus have a great deal in common.[29] Moral progress consists not so much in the discovery of ever higher standards as in
the extension of the group that constitutes the basic social unit.
For primitive man this is the family or the tribe. Later it becomes
the nation, and then an association of nations. Even the greatest
of Greek thinkers regarded all non-Greeks as barbarians, to be
treated as animals; the noble ethical systems of Plato and Aristotle were meant by their authors to be binding on Greeks only
in their dealings with other Greeks. It was Stoicism, followed
by Christianity, that first dared to state that the basic social unit
was the whole of humanity. But we have not yet assimilated that
teaching; in war, especially, the "enemy" is still to be treated as
"outside the pale."

A second point that the sociological relativists miss, though it
is established by their own investigations, is the fact that all men
everywhere and at all time make the distinction between right
and wrong and, apparently, cannot avoid doing so, no matter how
hard they may try. The significance of this universal distinction
remains, however different the specific kinds of acts labeled right
and wrong may be. The implication of this fact is that man as
such appears to be an incurably moral and value-making animal
—however mistaken his morality and values may be.

Every relativist on occasion slips into value-judgments. On one
page Brock Chisholm advocates the abolition of the terms
"right" and "wrong"[30]; on the next, he is inveighing against
the "wrongness" of war.[31] The greater part of Ruth Benedict's
Patterns of Culture is devoted to proving the relativity of all values. But in one extraordinary passage she passes a whole series
of value-judgments, thereby contradicting the very theory she is

defending. In this passage she says that the motive of rivalry that underlies American culture makes it " rank low in the scale of human values " (What scale and how can there be any " high " or " low " if there are no objective standards?). She then proceeds to speak of " all the virtues we prize in human life " (What virtues and who are the " we "?). She speaks of the possibility of " real improvements " in the social order (How can we know they are " improvements " unless we are acquainted with valid norms of social organization?). She says it is possible " to scrutinize different institutions and cast up their cost . . . in terms of the less desirable behavior traits they stimulate and in terms of human suffering and frustration " (Some behavior traits are " bad," then? Human suffering and frustration are " wrong "?). Finally, she says it in so many words: " We may train ourselves *to pass judgment* upon the dominant traits of our own civilization. . . . Any cultural control we may be able to exercise will depend upon the degree to which we can *evaluate objectively* the favored . . . traits of our Western civilization." [32] Here is the remarkable, but by no means unusual, spectacle of a complete relativist asserting the necessity of passing judgments and making objective evaluations. The point is, of course, that man must and does recognize some objectively valid criteria both for thought and for action; otherwise correct thinking and purposeful behavior would become impossible.

There is still another objection that we must make to complete relativism. If all standards are derived from some particular society, then three things follow: First, there can be no appeal against the existing social arrangements on the grounds that they are " unjust "; for, according to the theory of sociological relativism, the notion of what is " just " and " unjust " is altogether derived from the society in question. This means, secondly, that there can be no question of " improving " or " reforming " the given society, for the same reason. In this connection, it is worth noting that this kind of relativism, put into practice, could only encourage a kind of supine and apathetic conformity. The fact that sociological relativists are frequently in the van of reform movements, while a credit to their social zeal, is only one more illustration of the self-contradictory character of their relativism. Thirdly, if complete relativism is true, there can be no possibility of distinguishing in terms of value between one society and another: Nazism was just " right " for the Germans, Communism is " right " for the Russians, and democracy " right " for us. But none is objectively better or worse than the others. In the light of the historical experience of Nazism, such a position as this is surely untenable.

The conclusion to which these various criticisms of complete relativism point is that man is by nature a value-seeking animal and therefore cannot avoid making value-judgments. If this is a fact about human nature, it strongly suggests that there are objective values and moral standards and that it is possible for man to discover them. And this remains true, however much historical man may be conditioned in his judgments and in his pursuit of values by various physiological, sociological, and psychological factors. Finally, if there are such norms of human conduct and character, then, since these norms will define the good for man, it follows that the good life will consist, not in the unregulated and irrational expression of natural instinct and appetite, but rather in the realization in the individual and corporate life of these objective and universal values. In other words, there is no need to equate morality and values with authoritarian, repressive moralism. The occurrence and prevalence of a bad and unwholesome morality does not mean that there is no such thing as a good and healthy ethical system.

The " scientific " anthropology draws false conclusions from the genuine scientific evidence. On the basis of our scientific knowledge about the part that is played in human consciousness by the physical nervous system and brain, this anthropology gives " matter " the priority over " mind." On the basis of the theory of evolution, it asserts that man is nothing but a rather complicated animal. On the basis of the evidence provided by the social sciences and psychology, it pictures man as the slave of various material forces with his values and ends imposed upon him by irrational and impersonal factors.

This kind of materialism, determinism, and relativism deprive man of his humanity. They strip him of his specifically human and personal characteristics. They deny his spirit, his freedom, and his values. They reduce man entirely to the level of nature, regarding him as a mere thing or object, as " nothing but " a part of nature. Thus these doctrines prepare clients for totalitarianism, a system of absolute political control that puts these theories into actual practice.

The scientific evidence conclusively refutes the " religious " anthropology, with its body-soul dualism, its libertarianism, and its authoritarian moralism. But if, under the influence of scientism, this evidence is taken to be the whole truth about man, the result is a set of doctrines, at the opposite pole, that are equally false. The " scientific " anthropology with its one-level materialism, its absolute determinism, and its complete relativism is not the answer to the errors of the " religious " view. There must be a third alternative that can do justice to the scientific evidence without falling into the errors of the " scientific " anthropology.

CHAPTER VII

The Meaning of "Spirit"

BOTH THE "scientific" and the "religious" anthropologies, in spite of their errors, bear witness to authentic facts about the nature of man. The facts of which the "scientific" view takes account are those which are accessible to scientific investigation and are exhibited by the various sciences of man. Various forms of the "scientific" anthropology tend to go wrong in their exclusive preoccupation with the scientific evidence. At the same time some of these versions offer important clues to the solution of the problem of man's peculiar status in nature; and all of them do service as a counterbalance to the errors of the "religious" view.

The authentic facts about human nature attested by the "religious" anthropology are those that become apparent as soon as the "scientific" view is subjected to critical examination. The "religious" doctrine makes the mistake of exaggerating the difference between man and the rest of nature. At the same time, this anthropology serves to emphasize the fact that man is not simply reducible to the same level as the rest of nature, and that the reality of freedom and of universal norms cannot be denied without making nonsense of the whole human enterprise.

We are now in a position to state the major problem that confronts us in attempting to construct an anthropology that will do justice to all the facts. The problem is twofold: first, how to give full value to the scientific evidence about the nature of man, without slipping into the errors of the "scientific" anthropology, namely one-level materialism, absolute determinism, and complete relativism; and, second, how to explain man's transcendence over nature without falling back into the errors of the "religious" anthropology, namely, body-soul dualism, libertarianism, and absolutistic moralism. Man's undoubted transcendence over nature means that an adequate anthropology cannot dispense with the concepts of spirit, freedom, and values. On the other hand, the tremendous weight and power of the various material factors in shaping human life render untenable any form of dualism, libertarianism, and absolutism.

Interpretation of the Scientific Evidence

In examining the " scientific " doctrines of materialistic epiphenomenalism, determinism, and relativism, we stressed the fact that all of them contain important truths. These truths have to do with the facts, revealed by scientific investigation, about the way in which man thinks and acts.

The truth of epiphenomenalism resides in two facts: First, human consciousness is undoubtedly dependent in some sense on the physical nervous system and brain. Secondly, man's nature, including what we call his " mind," is unquestionably a product of natural evolution. These facts indicate that man is much more closely related to physical nature than the " religious " anthropology ever understood. On the other hand, neither of these facts has the slightest tendency to prove that " matter " is more real, more ultimate, or more important than " mind." What is the best way in which to describe the relationship between " mind " and " matter "?

The materialism of the Marxist philosophy appears to be very close to the truth, or at any rate to offer an important clue, when in the voice of Lenin it speaks of consciousness as " one of the properties of matter in motion," [1] a property that is " associated only with the higher forms of matter (organic matter) . . . with definite processes in matter organized in a definite way." [2] Lenin also, as we saw, hinted at the view that William Temple and others have since elaborated when he said that " in the foundation of the structure of matter we can only surmise the existence of a faculty akin to sensation." [3]

One-level materialism goes wrong in supposing that these facts somehow reduce " mind " to the level of " matter," or at least make " mind " inferior to " matter." In order to avoid this mistake we simply have to take evolution seriously, as a process of real *development*. If we take evolution seriously, then we shall have to emphasize both the continuity that obtains between all stages in the process and also the emergence, at various levels, of genuine novelties. These novelties are not extraneous insertions of new entities into the process, but are rather new developments of the same materials that have existed all along in the process. [4]

On the one hand, our emphasis on the continuity that exists between all stages in the process of evolution forbids our accounting for some new development, such as the appearance of man, by postulating the addition of a radically different ingredient or part, such as the rational soul. We must say, instead, that human life is continuous with, but distinct from, animal life, just as animal life is continuous with, but different from, the lower forms of living matter, and living matter continuous with, but different from, inanimate matter. In each case, the novelty or, better, the new development appears to consist in the fact, not that " something new has been added," but rather that a new and more complicated organization of the old elements has taken place. In this view, we can say, with Lenin, that human consciousness is a property of *matter organized in a definite way,* and is found only in association with matter so organized.

On the other hand, our emphasis on the emergence of real novelties or genuinely new developments will save us from the error of materialistic reduction. This error takes various forms. In one form, already noted, it is the mistake of assuming that once you have succeeded in tracing the development of a thing back to an earlier stage, you have thereby fully explained the later in terms of the earlier. But if real development is a fact, then this is clearly not the case. In the process of evolution, the same basic material ingredients are organized in ever new ways. And the increasingly complex and ever more highly organized wholes that result are genuinely new developments which cannot be reduced to the earlier levels. In the case of the human species we find matter organized into a new kind of whole such that it enjoys the " property " or faculty of rational consciousness.

Another form of the reductionist fallacy, the exposure of which is even more illuminating, is the assumption that any given whole is simply reducible to the sum of its parts. This presupposition is now widely questioned by scientists in many fields. Some biologists, for instance, insist that the examination of the constituent elements that make up a living organism is not enough by itself to enable us to appreciate the way in which the organism functions as a whole.[5] Similarly, Gestalt psychology emphasizes the fact that the over-all pattern of any psychical state is not simply reducible to its constituent elements. And the cultural anthropologist Ruth Benedict, with whom we have had to quarrel on another point, asserted in the strongest language that a given culture is always more than the set of particular customs and traits of which it consists; the cultural pattern or " configuration," she said, is a whole that is greater than the sum of its parts. She pointed out, further, that this is just one illustration, from the field of sociology, of a general truth that science in many fields is confirming.[6]

It may be that the familiar formula, " The whole is greater than the sum of its parts," is not altogether fortunate in its choice of words. It should not be understood as having any strange, " mystical " implications. It is simply a protest against the reductionist tendencies to which the exponents of analytical procedures are sometimes prone. The formula refers to the obvious fact that, in some cases at least, it is impossible to understand the functioning of the whole just by analyzing it into the functions of its constituent parts. One cannot, for instance, fully appreciate the first movement of a symphony, or the opening scenes of a novel, or the first stanzas of a poem, except in the context of the whole work. The general structure, the way in which the various parts are related to each other, gives their real meaning to the different elements in the composition. In the same way, human nature cannot be fully understood in terms of the material ingredients revealed by scientific analysis. The special abilities of man are functions of the whole organism and products of the way in which the various material constituents are organized — " matter organized in a definite way."

The most distinctive capacity of the whole we call " man " is a special type of consciousness. It is this, most of all, that differentiates human nature from the rest of nature, without breaking the continuous relationship that exists between the two. By virtue of the kind of consciousness he exercises, man is able to detach himself from nature sufficiently to observe it, to ask questions of it, to record its regularities, to predict its course, and so, within limits, to control it. In this sense, it seems indubitable that man is capable of transcending nature. And it is, of course, man's capacity for science among other things that bears witness to the reality of this kind of transcendence. Modern naturalism, with its devotion to science, must surely admit — and it can be shown that many versions of it do implicitly admit — the validity of this definition of the much-suspected term " transcendence."

Our argument is that an organism capable of knowing nature cannot be entirely reduced to the level of nature. To put it succinctly, that which does the knowing is not of the same order as that which is known. This dictum applies to man, not only in his relationship to external nature, but also in his relationship to his own nature. This is illustrated by the difficulty, already referred to, in which Freud was involved in his implied claim to have explained the whole inner nature of man. This claim cannot be made good, for obviously the act of knowing that enabled Freud to explain the psyche cannot itself be included in the psyche that is there explained. That which produces the explanation is not

itself explained by the explanation. If it were, then, since everything that occurs in the psyche tends to be regarded by Freud
as nothing but the precipitate of irrational forces, his own explanation of the psyche would have to be labeled "wishful thinking" or "rationalization." But Freud, of course, advanced his
views as a rational, objectively valid theory. This is only possible
if that which enabled Freud to explain the psyche transcends the
psyche that is being explained.

Our conclusion that man transcends nature, in the sense defined, does not, however, require us to postulate an independent
soul, different from the body and enabling him to exercise a
special type of consciousness. We are able to account for all the
facts if we say that in man the organization of the material elements is such that the resulting whole is capable of performing
activities like observing, recording, predicting, and controlling or,
in a word, knowing.

If it is true that man, in knowing nature, transcends nature,
we can see that this capacity involves the possibility of his exercising some kind of freedom in relation to nature. It is obvious
that prescientific man was the more or less helpless victim of natural forces precisely because of his ignorance. It is equally obvious
that the more man comes to know nature, the more he is freed
from servitude to natural forces and is enabled, to a considerable
extent, to master them. Because of his knowledge he is able to use
the forces of nature for his own purposes.

The fact that man, through knowledge, can control nature to
some extent does not mean, of course, that in discovering the
laws of nature he makes himself exempt from their operation. By
discovering certain laws of nature he learned how to fly; but he
did not thereby violate the law of gravity; he made use of it.
Similarly, advancing medical knowledge does not enable us to
disregard the operation of physiological laws; but it protects us
from many diseases, and cures many others, in the face of which,
in earlier times, men were more or less helpless. In the strictly

physical sphere, it is clear that our knowledge gives us a degree of mastery, and therefore of freedom, unknown in previous ages.

The social sciences and psychology, similarly, hold out the hope that man can attain the same kind of position in relation to the sociological and psychological forces to which he is exposed. As long as he is ignorant of social compulsions and psychical mechanisms, he is apt to be a more or less automatic product of these forces. But the more he comes to know the mechanics of society and psyche, the greater is the degree of his control and freedom in relation to them. Again it is true that knowledge of sociological and psychological laws does not exempt us from their operation; but it does enable us to make use of them for our own purposes. Further, as our knowledge in these areas increases, our purposes can be more and more deliberately chosen and no longer merely imposed upon us by the social environment and the mechanisms of the psyche.

Marx and Freud were pioneers in increasing our scientific knowledge of society and psyche. Since they, thereby, enhanced our freedom in relation to these powers, it is curious that they should have both been absolute determinists in theory. As a matter of fact, this paradox becomes quite explicit in the Marxist and Freudian writings. For while they insist on the doctrine of determinism, they also often speak of human freedom. It may be that what is involved in their determinism is just the denial of the *libertarian* conception of freedom, and that what they mean by "freedom" is something quite different from unrestricted freedom of choice. If so, then the so-called materialists may here also provide us with important clues.

The kind of freedom recognized by determinists as a real possibility is defined by Engels as "knowledge of necessity." In explaining his meaning, Engels went on to say that "freedom . . . means nothing but the capacity to make decisions with real knowledge." [7] In other words — and this is close to the view that we ourselves shall adopt — freedom is intimately related to a knowledge that embraces these physiological, sociological, and psychological forces that provide the limiting conditions of our human nature.

It is not only the economic determinist but also the psychological determinist who attaches great importance to this kind of freedom. For surely it is this that Freud must have had in mind when, in apparent contradiction of his " absolute psychical determinism," he said that it was the aim of psychoanalysis " to give the patient's ego freedom to choose." [8] It is a well-known fact that psychotherapy, largely by enabling the patient to know the nature and origin of his neurosis, hitherto buried in the unconscious, gives him a new freedom and mastery in relation to the mechanisms of his psyche. As the late David Roberts said, " It is as though a full awareness of what is involved in being in psychological fetters were a key that opens the door." [9]

Engels claimed that knowledge is freedom in the sense that it is the indispensable means to the accomplishment of our deliberate purposes. In one remarkable passage (remember that he called himself a determinist), he said that when we add the knowledge of social facts conveyed by the social sciences to the knowledge of nature given by the physical sciences,

" then, for the first time, man, in a certain sense, is finally marked off from the rest of the animal kingdom, and emerges from merely animal conditions of existence into really human ones. The whole sphere of the conditions of life which environ man, and which have hitherto ruled man, now comes under the dominion and control of man, who for the first time becomes the real, conscious lord of nature, because he has now become master of his own social organization. The laws of his own social action, hitherto standing face to face with man as law of nature foreign to and dominating him, will then be used with full understanding, and so mastered by him. Man's own social organization, hitherto confronting him as a necessity imposed by nature and history, now becomes the result of his own free action. The extraneous, objective forces that have hitherto governed history pass under the control of man himself. Only from that time will man himself, more and more consciously, make his own history — only from that time will the social causes set in movement by him, have in the main, and in constantly growing measure, the results intended by him. It is the ascent of man from the kingdom of necessity to the kingdom of freedom." [10]

For various reasons,[11] we should have to reject the excessive optimism of these predictions, but the main point would not be affected. Man's freedom resides, not in any alleged independence of all the various material factors, but rather in the capacity to *know* the nature and operation of these factors, and so to *use them for his own deliberate purpose.*

What we have been attempting to establish is that certain versions of naturalism actually recognize that it is man's special type of consciousness, issuing in knowledge, and his capacity for freedom inherent in this knowledge that have " finally marked him off from the rest of the animal kingdom " and constitute " the ascent of man from the kingdom of necessity to the kingdom of freedom." One could scarcely ask for a clearer statement of what we have called man's transcendence. And these assertions are made from within the naturalistic position itself.

Modern naturalism, at least in some of its forms, by no means entails the denial of human transcendence and freedom. The question of values, therefore, can be reopened. We have had occasion to notice that relativists are themselves unable at times to refrain from value-judgments, presumably assumed by them to be objectively valid. We can see now that, just as it is possible for man, through knowledge, to transcend nature, and in transcending it to gain a measure of freedom in relation to it, so also it is possible for him, in coming to know the facts of social and psychical organization, to achieve some degree of freedom in relation to these forces; and since these forces are the source of the conventional mores, imposed upon him unconsciously in the guise of absolute but pseudo values, it follows that freedom from such compulsions leaves the way open for the pursuit of genuine values.

As Engels said, man's knowledge enables him to use the laws

of social (and, we may add, psychological) action so that social (and psychical) developments will have " the results intended by him." Through his knowledge of social and psychical facts, man can make use of these forces for his own conscious and deliberate purposes. And these purposes that he now deliberately pursues are what he regards as good. In other words, they are his values, and these values no longer need be sociologically and psychologically determined; they can be consciously and deliberately chosen. This is certainly the implication of the word " freedom " where it occurs, as it does surprisingly often, in so much " deterministic " sociological and psychological literature. It follows, further, that if it is possible for man to choose his ends or " goods " deliberately, then there may be genuine and objective values, discoverable by him, as distinct from the relative and conventional standards that are imposed upon him by the pressures of society and the mechanisms of the psyche.

The upshot of this discussion is that some forms of so-called materialism, determinism, and relativism do not rule out the reality of the human spirit, human freedom, and human values. We must conclude that the " soul " denied by materialism is the misconceived " soul " of body-soul dualism, that the " freedom " rejected by determinism is the illusory " freedom " of the libertarian conception, and the " values " repudiated by relativism are the false absolutes of authoritarian moralism.

In all these denials and rejections, naturalism is perfectly correct. Moreover, it has some important positive truths to teach. The truth of materialism is that there is an inseparable interrelationship between the material bases of life and human consciousness in all its forms; man is a psychosomatic unity and not a composite creature consisting of two different substances. The truth of determinism is that the three sets of material factors, physiological, sociological, and psychological, perform an indispensable role in conditioning our beliefs, conduct, and way of life. The truth of relativism is that our values are usually, if not always, shaped into the precise form they take under the influence of these same forces. The truths of naturalism, however, by no means reduce man to the level of the rest of nature. To suppose that they do is the disastrous error into which the " scientific " anthropology is constantly falling. It is the mistake of first estimating and then treating man as though he were nothing but a part of nature — a thing or an object like everything else in nature.

Man undoubtedly is a part of nature — a thing or object like everything else in nature. But there are cogent reasons for insisting that he is not just a part of nature but also transcends nature. These reasons may be summarized as follows.

First, man is able, as the rest of nature is not, to achieve knowledge of nature — and also of his society and psyche. Because of his knowledge he is able in some degree to use these great powers for his own purposes, and not merely to be used by them. In this sense, and to this extent, he is capable of freedom. The faculty by which he gains this knowledge is commonly called the rational faculty. This is one of the means by which he transcends nature. And the reality of this kind of transcendence is recognized, as we have seen, by the most influential versions of modern naturalism, namely, those associated with the names of Marx and Freud.

Secondly, man is capable, as the rest of nature is not, of consciously and deliberately pursuing ends. These ends he regards as good; in other words, he is aware of values, and feels an obligation toward them. What the animal pursues is the gratification of immediate impulse and appetite, aroused by some immediate stimulus. Man, however, is able to envisage an object of desire not tied to the here and now — something neither spatially nor temporally present. In a word, man can desire something that *is not* but which he thinks *ought to be*. Further, what a man thinks ought to be is what he regards as good, and what he regards as good are his values, his values being the ultimate ends and purposes that he pursues in life. These values include not only moral goodness but also truth and beauty. It is not proper, therefore, to call the faculty in question simply the moral faculty. Since what is involved here is the endeavor after ends, we might call it the teleological faculty. It is a second way in which man transcends nature. And the reality of this mode of transcendence is attested by the fact that even the most extreme relativists are unable to refrain from making value-judgments.

Man enjoys (and suffers) a third capacity underlying, and therefore more fundamental than, the rational and teleological faculties. In fact, we now approach the key to the whole problem. This third capacity is the capacity for self-awareness. Man is, first of all, aware of himself as an individual, different and distinct from all other individuals, with the whole of nature over against him as an object. This kind of awareness enables him to observe and to know nature; it therefore makes him rational and is the basis of his rational faculty. Secondly, man is aware of himself as a *responsible* individual, bound to pursue what he regards as good — what he thinks ought to be — and obliged to refrain from what he thinks bad — what he thinks ought not to be. This kind of awareness drives him out in pursuit of the good; it therefore makes him teleological and is the basis of his teleological faculty.

It is human self-awareness, issuing in rational and teleological activities, that ultimately renders untenable a *one-level* materialism, an *absolute* determinism, and a *complete* relativism. At any rate, these doctrines must be rejected if they involve the denial of the human spirit, human freedom, and human values. The indubitable fact that man enjoys (and suffers) various modes of transcendence makes it impossible to dispense with these concepts in interpreting the heights and depths of the human situation.

MAN AS A SUBJECT

We must now attempt to define more precisely the meaning of these concepts "spirit," "freedom," "values." As we do so, we must bear in mind our central problem: how to do justice to the scientific evidence without slipping into the errors of the "scientific" anthropology; and how to explain man's transcendence and freedom without reverting to the errors of the "religious" anthropology. On the one hand, one-level materialism, absolute determinism, and complete relativism must be rejected. On the other hand, dualism, libertarianism, and absolutism must be avoided.

We shall begin by examining the meaning of "spirit" as applied to man. Here we must avoid both the dualism that thinks of the spirit or soul of man as a kind of independent substance, and also the one-level materialism that reduces man entirely to the level of nature.

The clue to the solution of this problem lies in a vitally important distinction. This is the distinction between subject and object.[12] Science, by its very nature, is concerned with objects. It began as a method of investigating the external world — the realm of objects and of things — in which fixed laws appear to prevail. Because of the great success, in terms of knowledge and power, achieved by science in this area, it gradually came to be assumed that the whole of reality, including human nature in all its aspects, could be exhaustively explained in this way. Man, it was thought, could be completely understood by means of categories appropriate to the external world. Freud, for example, claimed it as one of the great virtues of his hypothesis that it enabled him to "establish psychology upon foundations similar to those of any other science."[13] Similarly, Auguste Comte liked to describe his social theories as "social physics."[14] In the same way, we frequently encounter in sociological literature the phrase "social engineering." When studies of the human being and of human society are thus modeled on the physical sciences, the danger is that man will be regarded as nothing but a part of nature, as merely an object or a thing, like everything else in nature. This is what Arnold Toynbee has labeled " the apathetic fallacy," the error of applying to " a study of living creatures a scientific method devised for the study of inanimate nature." [15]

As we have seen, man is a part of nature, and therefore a thing and an object. But he is not merely a part of nature. His self-awareness, making rational reflection and control possible, and enabling him to act purposefully in pursuit of deliberately chosen ends, means that in some sense he transcends nature. As an organism that is aware of himself, man is a center of consciousness, an observing, knowing, and controlling self, a purposive agent. He is not *just* an object; he is a *self-conscious* object. And this is precisely what we mean by the category of " subject."

In more traditional language, we might say that man is not just a thing but also a person, or not just an " it " but also an " I." This is also the real significance of that kind of " religious " language which says that man has a " spiritual " as well as a purely material status, or that he is a citizen of two worlds, or that he stands on the boundary between the natural and the " supernatural " — or even that he has a " soul " as well as a body.

In fact, the danger of all the traditional language, which tries to do justice to man's special status, is that it is apt to mislead us in the direction of the old " religious " anthropology. It is better, therefore, to find new terms and to speak, not of " matter " and " spirit " or " matter " and " mind " or " natural " and " supernatural " [16] or " body " and " soul," but rather of " object " and " subject." But whenever we say that man is a subject as well as an object, we must be careful to make plain that we do not mean that in addition to the objective aspects of his being — the sum total of all the material factors that compose his nature — there is another part or substance in man that we call his " ego " or his " real self." We mean, rather, that in this case all the material factors are organized in a special way, so as to produce a unique kind of object, namely, a self-conscious object, that is to say a subject.

Man is, first of all, an object, a part of nature. His being is formed and constituted by three main sets of material factors: the strictly physical, studied by the physical and biological sciences; the social, studied by the social sciences; and the psychical, studied by the science of psychology. Man is an organized whole, consisting of these material ingredients. But on the higher levels of organization the whole structure cannot be fully understood simply as a collection of parts. The distinctive functions and characteristics of the entity belong to the structure as a whole and depend upon its special type of organization. In the case of the human being, the structure of the material factors is such that the resulting whole exercises a special type of consciousness. The defining characteristic of this type of consciousness is its *self*-consciousness. It is his self-consciousness that makes man a knowing and purposive agent. This is what we mean when we say that man not only possesses the status of an object, like other wholes in nature, but also enjoys and suffers the status of a subject. It is this *status* that is the real referent of the terms " spirit " and " spiritual," as applied to human nature.

It is now possible for us to give a summary analysis of man's nature as we see it. We can follow the well-established tradition, as ancient as Plato and as modern as Freud, of making a threefold distinction. In the first place, we recognize the strictly physical constituents of man's being. Secondly, we can group together, as all quasi-physical, those aspects of human nature that are studied by the social sciences and psychology, and we can call these the sociopsychological factors. And in the third place, avoiding the term " subjective " because of its undesirable connotations, we shall make use of what appears to be the only available alternative and speak of the spiritual dimension in human life.

In making this threefold distinction between the physical, the sociopsychological, and the spiritual, there are two important points to which we must pay special attention. In the first place, we should notice that the last of these terms belongs to a quite different category from the first two. The terms " physical " and " sociopsychological " refer to various material constituents of man's nature, while the term " spiritual " refers to the way in which these constituents are organized to make up the whole. The " spirit " is nothing apart from these physical and sociopsychological elements, but the former is not therefore reducible to the latter. Another way of stating this distinction would be to say that the category of the physical and sociopsychological embraces the objective elements in man's nature, while the category of spirit refers to man's status as a subject.

This kind of analysis permits us to say, with certain qualifications to be noted immediately, that the physical sciences deal with the physical level of man's being, and the social and psychological sciences with the sociopsychological factors, but that science is not able to deal directly with the third or spiritual dimension. It certainly does *not,* however, allow us to assign the third dimension by itself to "religion." This neat and popular division of labor, handing over the physical and quasi-physical to science and retaining the spiritual for "religion," simply will not work. And one of the reasons it will not work is that the third or spiritual dimension is not a *tertium quid* at all but has to do with the whole man. Therefore, on the one side, the sciences, by analyzing the various material factors, contribute to our understanding of the whole; so that it is not altogether true to say that science does not deal with the spiritual. On the other side, true religion, just because it is concerned with the spirit of man, is necessarily interested in the whole man; so that it is not at all true to say that religion has nothing to do with the physical and sociopsychological aspects of human nature.

The second point to be emphasized affords another reason for rejecting the spurious division of labor between science and religion. The three dimensions of man's nature are not separate and independent parts, but closely interrelated and overlapping aspects. It is impossible anywhere to draw fixed lines or establish firm boundaries. This fact is illustrated in the scientific study of man by the emphasis on the psychosomatic point of view. The sciences of man know very well that the *sōma* and the *psychē* are not different entities. For science, man is a psychosomatic organism, within which the physical and the psychical may be distinguished for analysis but not separated in fact. Similarly, when we claim that the category of the physical and sociopsychological does not exhaust the depth of man's nature, we are not suggesting that in addition to the *sōma* and the *psychē* there is a third part called the *pneuma*. On the contrary, we are saying that man is not only a psychosomatic organism or object, but also a self-conscious psychosomatic organism or subject. And our three aspects of human nature are not separable in fact but only distinguishable for analysis.

It is because of the possibility of distinguishing these three dimensions, and also because of the nature of our language, that we naturally tend to employ nouns in this connection and to speak of "body," "soul," and "spirit," or of "matter," "mind," and "spirit." But this linguistic usage can involve us in consequential mistakes. It can lead to reification, tending to imply that the three nouns in question stand for three different substances. In fact, the concepts of "body," "soul," and "spirit," like "mind" and "matter," are in themselves more or less artificial abstractions. They are abstracted from what is in reality an undivided whole. When we use these nouns, we should therefore put them in quotation marks.

The use of nouns in this context is a fruitful source of what Gilbert Ryle calls "category mistakes,"[17] the tendency to use two different sets of terms as though they belonged to the same logical category, when in fact they belong to two different categories. He ascribes this "myth of the ghost in the machine," or body-soul dualism, to a mistake of this kind. In this myth, the term "soul" is used as though it belonged to the same logical category as the term "body," as though the "soul" were really the same sort of thing as the body, only more refined, a kind of ghostly counterpart of the body. This is comparable to supposing that the term "team" belongs to the same category as the term "players," as though after inspecting all the players, one might then ask, "But where is the team?" The team, of course, is not something that exists in addition to the players; it *is* the players, organized in a certain way. Similarly, the "soul," in the sense of "spirit," is not something over and above the material constituents of human nature; it *is* these material constituents, organized in a definite way.

However, if the "religious" anthropology is guilty of confusing logically different categories, the "scientific" view makes the mistake of assuming that there is only one valid category. Here the only category that is recognized is the category of objects. Ryle himself, in his very proper desire to expose the errors of body-soul dualism, often leaves the impression that he has reacted to the opposite and equally indefensible extreme of behaviorism.[18] The mistake that behaviorism makes is to try to translate all sentences pertaining to activities appropriate to subjects into sentences about the behavior of objects. In other words, the only category it has at its disposal is the category of objects. But, we may well inquire of Ryle, If there is only one category, how can a "confusion" of categories arise? The opponents of body-soul dualism too often fail to notice that the theory they are attacking is a mistaken attempt to do justice to genuine facts. If it is a mistake to suppose that the team is something over and above its members, it is just as much a mistake to assume that, because the team is nothing apart from its members, it is therefore nothing at all. Any team that is worth its salt is a good deal more than a mere collection of individuals. It is the same kind of mistake to suppose that, because the "spirit" is nothing apart from its material constituents, it is therefore nothing at all.

The term " spirit " in our anthropology refers to the fact that man is a self-conscious psychosomatic organism or subject. This is what differentiates him from the objects that compose the rest of nature. These objects are either inorganic (such as atoms) or living organisms (plants) or psychosomatic organisms (animals). As a psychosomatic organism, man is an object and a part of nature. But as a self-conscious psychosomatic organism, he is a subject and transcends nature. He transcends nature in the sense that he is able to think about it and control it, to pursue deliberate purposes, to recognize authentic values, and to feel legitimate obligation.

This distinction between subject and object, establishing the real meaning of " spirit," enables us to account for all the facts without slipping into either an oversimplified materialism or a naïve dualism.

Causes and Conditions

We must next attempt to clarify the real meaning of " freedom." Here the opposite errors to be avoided are, on the one hand, an absolute determinism and, on the other, an unrealistic libertarianism. Absolute determinism misinterprets the role of the material factors in human life, while libertarianism misunderstands the nature of man's transcendence. Once again, it is a fundamentally important distinction that can help us to avoid these dangers and solve this problem.

The way out of the impasse was suggested long ago by Socrates in a well-known passage in *Phaedo*. The scene of this dialogue is Socrates' prison cell, where he is awaiting execution as the result of the sentence passed upon him by an Athenian jury. He has decided to remain in jail and accept the verdict, though it is quite possible for him to escape at any time. His friends have made all the arrangements and the authorities would be only too glad to be rid of their embarrassing prisoner. It is against this background that Socrates now raises the question, Why is Socrates sitting here at this moment? Some would say that the cause of his sitting here is the particular disposition of his bones, muscles, and sinews. But surely, says Socrates, this is an absurdly inadequate " explanation." The real cause of Socrates' sitting here is his decision that it is right for him to obey the laws and to accept the verdict of the society from which he has benefited all his life long. To be sure, he adds, Socrates could not continue to sit here and carry out his decision unless the various parts of his body were arranged in the appropriate way. But these physiological factors are the conditions and not the cause of his sitting here. The real cause is the conscious and deliberate choice that he has made in accordance with what he thinks good.[19]

We can apply this Socratic distinction between conditions and causes to the solution of our problem: how to do justice to the part that is played by material factors in shaping human life without succumbing to some untenable form of determinism, and how to recognize the reality of human freedom without relapsing into a discredited libertarianism. We can now say that the whole vast, complicated machinery of material forces, physical, social, and psychical, constitute the inescapable material conditions, differing more or less from man to man, within which every one of us must do his thinking, perform his actions, and develop his character. The individual cannot avoid their influence or operate independently of them. These material conditions set certain limits, and mark out the general lines, within which his growth takes place. They provide a more or less fixed framework within which he must think and do and become whatever it is that he thinks and does and becomes. But wherever the activity in question is specifically human, and not merely a relapse to the animal level, then all these material factors, massive and potent as they are, are the limiting conditions and not the real cause of the occurrence. The real cause is the conscious decision made in accordance with a deliberate purpose.

The distinction that we have expressed as existing between "causes" and "conditions" can be stated in other ways. Aristotle had the same point in mind when he differentiated between "final causes" and "efficient causes." A third kind of terminology makes the contrast in terms of "teleological" and "mechanical" causes. However we express it, the distinction is of fundamental significance. Man can act, not only as a result of material conditions or efficient and mechanical causes, pushing him from behind (so to speak), but also as a result of real or final or teleological causes, pulling him from in front. And these final causes, or purposes, are not themselves just reducible to material conditions; they need not be the haphazard and more or less unconscious ends that his society pursues. This may usually be the case; but it is not necessarily the case. For man enjoys a special type of consciousness and is capable of knowledge. And since he can come to know the forces of nature, the pressures of society, and the mechanisms of his psyche, then, without ceasing to be conditioned by them, he nonetheless transcends them. This is "the ascent of man from the kingdom of necessity to the kingdom of freedom."

It is because man is a knowing subject, as well as a known object, that he can act with conscious and deliberate purpose. He can act in pursuit of ends that he thinks good, that is to say, in pursuit of values. And what he thinks good need not be entirely determined by sociopsychological pressures. In so far as he is capable, through knowledge, of transcending these irrational forces, he is able, within limits, to seek out and discover objective values. It is true that the various material factors constituting his nature will always condition the way in which he formulates his values, so that he is never in possession of pure goodness or beauty itself or of absolute truth. He cannot act or think apart from the limiting conditions of his being. But on those occasions, perhaps few in number, when he is acting as a human person and a knowing subject, and not merely behaving as an object or a thing, then it is he that makes use of these material factors and not they that make use of him. Ultimately, in so far as he achieves the status of a subject, the limiting conditions of his existence are not responsible for what he thinks and does and becomes. He is responsible for the use that he makes of the materials given to him. Remember the parable of the talents (Matt. 25:14 ff.).

Spirit, freedom, and values are all realities. It was the glory of the "religious" anthropology that it bore witness to them, but in witnessing to them it misconceived them, so that, for all its good intentions, it succeeded only in bringing them under suspicion. This suspicion has been confirmed by the evidence amassed in the various sciences of man. On the other hand, those who are impressed by this evidence and repelled by the errors of "religion" are tempted to elaborate a "scientific" anthropology that ignores or denies the farthest reaches of man's being. Over against both these views we have attempted to suggest an anthropology that takes account both of the deeper realities recognized by religion and the plain facts discovered by science.

APPENDIX TO CHAPTER VII: GOD AS "SPIRIT"

The conception of "spirit" that I have suggested in this chapter has implications for the understanding of God conceived of as "spirit." Corresponding to the radical body-soul dualism of the "religious" view of man, there is a crude supernaturalism that thinks of God as altogether "outside" the world and "above" the whole realm of matter. This conception of the divine transcendence seems to me to be a mistake of the same kind as the dualistic interpretation of man's transcendence over nature. It is all of a piece with the view that identifies spirit in general with the otherworldly and the non-material.

It would seem to me far better to approach the question of God and his relation to the world by way of any analogy based on the interpretation of the human spirit and its relation to the material basis of life, such as I have suggested here. The term "spirit" as applied to man does not refer to some alleged part of his being separate from and superior to his body. It refers to man's special status as a subject and a person. Because of the type of consciousness that man enjoys and suffers, he can become aware of himself and can come to know and purposefully to control nature, within limits. This constitutes his transcendence over nature. Similarly, when we say that God is spirit and ascribe personality to him, we do not mean that he is a kind of supernatural man, in the sense of a sort of superthing over and above the world. We mean that his relationship to nature and the world is analogous to man's relationship to nature and to the material basis of his existence. Just as in the case of man, so in the case of God, his transcendence has nothing to do with separation but is related to the capacity for knowledge of and purposive control over nature. And in both cases this kind of transcendence is perfectly consistent with immanence.

On the other hand, just as man's transcendence over nature means that he cannot be entirely reduced to the level of nature, as some forms of naturalism suggest, so also God's transcendence over nature means that he cannot be simply identified with nature, as pantheistic naturalism seems to argue. At the same time, we have to admit that this kind of pantheism is understandable as a protest against crude supernaturalism, just as naturalism itself is justified, to some extent, as a protest against radical dualism.

It is perhaps necessary to emphasize that I have here been making use of an analogy. The terms " spirit " and " personality " cannot be applied univocally to man and God. If there is a real difference in status between things in nature and human persons, there is no doubt a much vaster difference between men and God. For one thing, the self-awareness, knowledge, and power that constitute the meaning of " spirit " are limited in man, whereas they are complete in God, so that his knowledge is omniscience and his power omnipotence. For another thing, the sinfulness of man constantly corrupts his purposes, whereas the holiness of God means that his purposes are good without qualification.

Doubtless the idea of God that I have here barely sketched in will be called in question on the score of orthodoxy. In replying to such criticism, I would only suggest further reflection on the meaning of the Holy Spirit, the Logos doctrine, the sacramental view of the relation between spirit and matter, and the insistence on the immanence, as well as the transcendence, of God, all of which are standard in Christian theology. I would also appeal for support to two of the most eminent of twentieth century theologians, belonging to two quite different Christian traditions, namely William Temple and Karl Heim. As I understand them, both have a conception of God that is not different, in any essential respect, from the one I have suggested. (See Temple, *Nature, Man and God* [The Macmillan Company, London, 1935], Chs. X and XI; and Heim's *Christian Faith and Natural Science* [Harper & Brothers, New York, 1953], II, 11–12, and III, 13–18.)

This is not the place to enlarge on theology proper. I am concerned here only to show that the concepts of spirit, personality and transcendence, in the case of both man and God, do not necessarily imply any radical dualism in anthropology or any crude supernaturalism in theology. It may be that in attempting this reconstruction I have succeeded only in offending both the scientists and the theologians, both the naturalists and the supernaturalists. But that may be unavoidable.

PART THREE

The Biblical View of Man

PART THREE

The Biblical View of Man

CHAPTER VIII

The Biblical Attitude
to the Physical

THE " RELIGIOUS " ANTHROPOLOGY, as far as Western
thought is concerned, is Greek and not Biblical in origin. It is
also typical of Eastern religions in general, such as Hinduism and
Buddhism. It seems to be characteristically " religious," and for
this and other reasons has tended to creep into and corrupt the
Christian view of man. This happened, as we saw, in the patristic
and medieval periods, and modern Catholicism and Protestantism
have tended to perpetuate this early mistake. Modern secular
thought has tended, until fairly recently, in the same direction,
because of its Renaissance and Cartesian background.

Recently, however, under the weight of the evidence collected
by the various sciences, secular thought has altogether rejected the
" religious " anthropology and has reacted to the opposite extreme. The resulting " scientific " anthropology commits the same
sort of mistakes as the " religious," only at the opposite extreme.
While the one view deifies the " soul " and thinks of it as quite
other than and independent of the body, the other denies that the
concept of " spirit " has any meaning at all. While the one claims
for the independent " soul " an unlimited power to choose, the
other insists that man has no freedom at all. And while the ascetic moralism of the one view, contemptuous of and hostile to
the physical in general, adopts a repressive and authoritarian
ethics, the relativism of the other rejects all objective norms and
advocates the uninhibited expression of natural impulses.

Both these anthropologies, standing at opposite extremes, can be shown to be mistaken in detail. Each nonetheless stands for important truths about human nature that the other rejects or ignores. The " religious " anthropology is right when it opposes the attempted reductions of naturalism and insists on the reality of spirit, freedom, and values in human life. The " scientific " anthropology is right when it exposes the mistakes of the other position and emphasizes the importance of the various material factors in shaping the nature of man. In the previous chapter we have attempted to show how both sets of truths can be combined in an authentic and comprehensive anthropology.

It now remains to establish two points: first, that the Biblical view of man is entirely different from the " religious "; and, secondly, that while the scientific evidence undoubtedly refutes the latter, it in no way contradicts the former.

The Old Testament Attitude to the Physical

It is perhaps necessary to begin here by reminding ourselves of the exclusiveness of the Old Testament position vis-à-vis the various religions of the time. The strange insistence that Israel was the chosen people stands for this fact, at any rate, that their conception of God and the world was sharply distinguished from the typical beliefs of contemporary religion. The Israelites, of course, were constantly tempted, like their Christian successors, to slip into the errors of neighboring religions. It is against this temptation, commonly called " idolatry," that the prophets are always inveighing.

The fact that this sin was known as idolatry shows that the efforts of the prophets were chiefly directed at preserving the distinctiveness and purity of the Hebrew conception of God. But the conception of God never stands by itself; it always has important implications for the conception of man and the world.[1] Thus, the peculiar convictions about the nature of God, embraced by Israel, were accompanied by peculiar ideas about man and the world.

We pointed out earlier[2] that the "religious" anthropology appears to belong to one stage in the normal development of "religion," and that the Hebrews never seem to have passed through this phase. This is our justification for calling this anthropology "religious" and also for hesitating to apply that adjective to the Biblical teaching.

The Biblical anthropology is distinctive because, as we have already implied, the Biblical theology is distinctive. And the link between this peculiar conception of God and this peculiar conception of man is a peculiar conception of the world. The Biblical estimate of the whole realm of matter is entirely different from the Greek and Eastern view. Where the latter depreciates and even vilifies the physical, as more or less unreal and definitely evil, the former insists that the whole material order, as created by God, is both real and good.

It is in the Genesis story of creation that the Biblical cosmology, or attitude to the physical, is first of all manifested. We shall examine this story from a theological, rather than from a literary or critical, point of view. It is well known that the first three chapters of Genesis have been assembled from two stories belonging to two different periods. But they were put together for theological purposes to form one story. And since our interests here are also theological, we can ignore the problem of sources and treat the Genesis story of creation as though it were one story. This story contains three important points.

In the first place, the story tells us that matter was created by God. It is not something that he is confronted with and with which he has to wrestle, as with something recalcitrant and bad. In the "religious" view, wherever there is a creation story, as in Plato's *Timaeus,* it is regularly phrased in these latter terms. But the Biblical story, while it is clearly derived from typical "religious" myths, probably Babylonian in origin, is sharply distinguished from the normal "religious" view precisely by the eradication, no doubt deliberate, of the characteristic "religious" elements. In the Genesis story God is absolutely Creator; he does not merely shape and mold a pre-existent matter that resists his will.

In the second place, the whole material order, as created by God, was created for a purpose, and has an eternal place in God's plans. This is one of the plain implications in the story. The Creator is a purposive being. He does not act arbitrarily or haphazardly. Everything that he creates has a place in his eternal purpose. This is true of the whole physical order, including the human " body " with its desires and instincts. It is not something ultimately to be annihilated by God and escaped from by man; it has eternal significance.

Thirdly, it follows from the fact that the physical was created in accordance with the divine purpose that the physical in general is good. For, as we have seen,[3] " purpose " and " good " are almost synonymous terms. Certainly on the Biblical presuppositions, the purposes of God are identical with the good; they constitute the objective and universal values. Thus, both our second and third points are asserted in the verse, " And God saw every thing that he had made, and, behold, it was very good " (Gen. 1:31). There could be no clearer declaration than this, in the very first chapter of the Bible, that the physical, including man's " body " and all that goes with it, is not insignificant and bad, as in the " religious " view, but is rather, in itself and as created by God, of fundamental importance and goodness. The Bible at the outset rules out the " religious " denigration of the physical and the " puritanical " hostility to the body and its natural appetites.

On the basis of the Biblical story of creation, then, we can say that in this view the material order is God's creation, that it has an eternal place in his purposes, and that it is good.

It is relevant also to point out here that in the creation story man is made both " of the dust of the ground " (Gen. 2:7) and also " in the image of God " (ch. 1:27). We shall later give a fuller interpretation of the meaning of these words, but we can say now that they preclude both the "religious" view that man has a divine element in him, and also the "scientific" view that deprives him of his spirit. Both passages make it clear that in this view man has no divine element in him. There is no part of man that is of divine origin and that comes down to take up temporary residence in the alien "body." Man in no way participates in the divine nature. He is made of the dust of the ground, and his relationship to God is not that of a spark to the fire or a drop of water to the ocean but rather that of an image to its original. Thus there is nothing in man that establishes an identity or even a continuity between him and God, as the rational "soul" does in the "religious" view. Instead of identity, there is merely likeness; instead of continuity, there is radical discontinuity, as between creature and Creator.

The only mention of "soul" in the story occurs in the Greek and English translations of one verse: "God . . . breathed into his nostrils the breath of life; and man became a living soul" (ch. 2:7). The Hebrew word translated "soul" is *nephesh*. This word has scarcely any of the connotations of the word "soul" in radical body-soul dualism. Certainly, it does not mean the rational and divine "soul" of the fully developed "religious" anthropology. *Nephesh* is applied to animal life elsewhere in the Old Testament (Gen. 7:22). It is applicable to any living thing; it means simply "life-breath." It is not this "life-breath," then, that differentiates man from the rest of nature. Nonetheless, he most definitely is distinguished from everything else in creation, according to this story. The alternative to body-soul dualism is not one-level materialism or crude naturalism. What distinguishes man from the rest of nature is that he is made in "the image of God." As we shall see later, this means that there are inherent in human nature godlike possibilities. By virtue of the way in which he is created by God, man is capable of achieving a personal status that is akin to the life of God.

We turn next to the Biblical account of the way in which man has used and abused these God-given potentialities. The story of the "Fall" of Adam and Eve in Genesis is the Old Testament attempt to come to grips with the problem of evil in human life. This is the same problem that the "religious" anthropology tried to solve by identifying matter as the source and origin of evil. In this way it avoided assigning the responsibility for evil to God; for matter was independent of the Creator. On the other hand, this identification of evil with matter involved a hatred of the "body" as the source of sin and a conception of earthly existence as an unmitigated disaster — as one long, miserable expiation or prison sentence. Now, of course, the fact of evil in human life is undeniable, and as a result it is true that earthly existence is full of pain and tears. A realistic view of man inevitably involves some kind of radical pessimism. This is the genuine fact to which the "religious" view bears witness, albeit a false witness. The pessimistic estimate of human life on earth is by no means unfounded. But the "religious" view wrongly identifies the source of evil and suffering with the physical basis of life.

Now in the story of Adam and Eve, which we shall interpret more fully later on,[4] there is not the slightest tendency to pin the blame for evil on matter or the physical, either in reality in general or in man in particular. How could there be, in view of the fact that the story of Adam and Eve, intended to explain the origin of evil in human life, immediately follows the story of the creation by God of the whole physical order? Some commentators [5] on the third chapter of Genesis, have indeed interpreted the story of the Fall as though the sin of Adam and Eve consisted of an illicit act of sexual intercourse. There is no ground whatever in the text itself for this kind of exegesis. In the context it is fantastic. The temptation to which Adam and Eve listened and yielded was not the temptation to indulge in any physical desire of any kind. The temptation was, "Ye shall be as gods" (Gen. 3:5). The sinfulness of man, the origin of evil in human life, has nothing at all to do with the "body" or with the physical in general. It resides, rather, in the fact that man, just because he is made in the image of God, is constantly tempted to act as though he were God. He is always putting himself, instead of God, in the center of everything.

In the Biblical view, then, the origin of evil in life, or " original sin " (a phrase that does not occur in the Bible), is not to be located in some specific act, committed long ago, or in some particular class of acts to which man is prone. The source of evil or " original sin " is a certain condition or state of life. Man is in a sinful condition because his life is self-centered; and this means that his life is off center, misoriented. Because of this misorientation at the roots of human nature, everything in human life tends to go wrong. The tremendous possibilities for good, inherent in human nature and represented in the story by " the image of God " in man, are realized in the course of human development in a disastrously wrong way. What are godlike potentialities become demonic actualities.

We shall have to return to this subject in our last chapter. Suffice it to say now that we have only to recognize the use that man has made of his knowledge, power, and freedom in order to realize that some deep and terrible corruption has entered into man's heart and has prevented him from becoming what God meant him to be — a real person reflecting the glory of the divine personality.

Thus, the Biblical aetiology, given in the Old Testament story of creation and the " Fall," is radically different from the characteristic Orphic aetiology of the " religious " anthropology. In the Old Testament, there is no tendency to regard matter as evil; it is created by God and is good. There is no tendency to regard man as a composite being, consisting of a divine, immortal soul that comes down from the eternal, heavenly realm and a mean, perishing body that belongs to an inferior level of reality. On the contrary, man is made of the dust of the ground, with the breath of life breathed into it but, more important, with the image of his Creator stamped on his nature. Nor is there any tendency to locate the source of evil in the " body " and its appetites. The origin of evil in human life is located in the tendency, possible only for a being made in the image of God, to act and to think of himself as though he were God; to assume, in the words of C. S. Lewis, the status of a noun when he is really only an adjective. This means that the whole of human life is thrown off its true axis; all elements in man's nature, the spiritual and rational as well as the physical and material, become in a subtle way perverted. It means that men do not become what they were meant to be, sons of God enjoying " the glorious liberty of the children of God " (Rom. 8:21); they become, instead, sons of perdition enslaved in the terrible " bondage of corruption."

THE NEW TESTAMENT ATTITUDE TO THE PHYSICAL

Our examination of the Old Testament estimate of the physical in general has concluded with some phrases borrowed from the New Testament. This is appropriate enough, for the New Testament maintains the Old Testament attitude on this point. This is clear enough in its central doctrine of the incarnation. The Gospel According to St. John announces that the eternal Word or Logos, which " in the beginning was . . . with God . . . and . . . was God . . . was made flesh and dwelt among us " (John 1:1 ff.). The very idea that the eternal should enter time and space and should assume a full human nature, including a " body," was entirely foreign to the Greek mind. This illustrates, with the utmost force, the difference between the Biblical point of view and the " religious " metaphysics. Anyone who understands the meaning of the New Testament doctrine of the incarnation can never accuse the New Testament writers of any attempt to denigrate, much less vilify, the physical order. The importance and dignity of the body, along with the whole material realm, is an undoubted implication of this teaching.

A second central declaration of the gospel has to do with the purpose of the incarnation. And this purpose contains the same implication. The same eternal Word, which being spoken in the beginning created the world, now came into the world to recreate it. He came to renew and redeem not just the " soul," but the whole of the world; not just the " soul," but the whole of man.

This is the significance of the strange doctrine of the resurrection of the body which more than anything else horrified and repelled the Greek world. This doctrine served to emphasize, in the strongest possible way, the New Testament view that it is not some part of man (his rational " soul ") that is destined for fulfillment in eternity; it is the whole person that has his place in God's purposes. The " body," the physical structure and all the material factors that play their part in shaping the life of the individual, does not constitute an inferior " part " of man, to be discarded at death so that the pure " spirit " can escape to some higher, celestial realm of blessedness. On the contrary, the " body " has its eternal significance in the divine scheme of things.

This implication can be drawn from the New Testament teaching only if it can be shown that in the new Testament the resurrection body is in some sense the same " body " as our present " body." Such an interpretation is necessary to our whole thesis and must therefore be substantiated. Some theologians maintain that the resurrection body cannot be regarded as a " body " in the ordinary sense at all. They point to Saint Paul's statement that " flesh and blood cannot inherit the kingdom " (I Cor. 15:50) and to his description of the resurrection body as a " spiritual body " (I Cor. 15:44).[6] They cite the verse, " For we know that, if our earthly house of this tabernacle were dissolved, we have . . . a house not made with hands, eternal in the heavens " (II Cor. 5:1). These passages are taken to prove that the resurrection " body " is an entirely new " body " and bears no relation to the old whatever; it can be called a " body " only in the sense that it is an instrument and expression of the " spirit," and not in any " crudely materialistic " sense.

If this were the case, then one of the central parts of our case would collapse; the material factors of our present existence would have no eternal significance. Fortunately, however, a different exegesis of the passages in question is entirely possible. The explanation of the first two references depends on the interpretation of the Pauline antithesis between the " flesh " and the " spirit." We hope to show in detail, later on,[7] that " flesh " is by no means to be identified with " body," nor " spiritual " with " nonmaterial." As for the third passage, J. A. T. Robinson has argued convincingly that the " house not made with hands, eternal in the heavens " does not refer to the individual resurrection body to be received at the last day, but rather to the " body of Christ," the Church which is a present reality. After all, Saint Paul does say, " We *have* . . . a house "; it would be bizarre indeed to suppose that multitudes of " resurrection bodies " are now waiting in heaven to be allotted at the last day to the individuals for whom they are destined.[8]

The *locus classicus* of the Pauline teaching on the resurrection is I Cor., chapter 15. There the relation between the present " body " and the resurrection body is likened to that between a seed and the full-grown plant. This relation is one of potentiality to actuality and assumes an essential identity and continuity, along with radical change and fulfillment. This interpretation is confirmed by the strongest evidence we have for the New Testament teaching on this question, namely, the way in which the resurrection body of Jesus himself is described. It was obviously the same body; the disciples recognized him (Matt. 28:9; Luke 24:31; John 20:16, 20); they touched him (John 20:24 ff.); he ate with them and was anxious to assure them that he was not a " spirit " (Luke 24:36 ff.). On the other hand, it was the same " body " with a difference; the disciples did not always recognize him directly or easily (Luke 24:16; John 20:11 ff.); he passed through closed doors and did not seem to be subject to the ordinary laws of space and time (Luke 24:36; John 20:19).

We have to conclude that in the New Testament view the resurrection body is the same " body," but the same " body " changed in various ways and brought to its perfection.

Similarly, in the New Testment eschatology, the whole physical realm has its place in the final consummation. This earth is the locale of the working out of God's purposes for man; like the " body," therefore, it too has an eternal significance. It is not a temporary prison house or proving ground for " souls," destined for ultimate annihilation. This earth will be the scene of the consummation of God's plan for humanity. In this connection, it is worth remembering that the Old Testament hope for the future is extremely " materialistic." Apart from a few passages in the Apocrypha (e.g., Wisdom of Solomon 3:1-9; 9:15), clearly influenced by Greek ideas, there is no mention of the typically " religious " notion of the immortality of the detachable soul. On this point, as on so many, the Hebrew ideas were not at all " religious." While Orphism, Greek philosophy, and Eastern religions were looking forward to the " soul's " eventual escape from this earth into the ethereal regions, the Hebrews were awaiting the establishment of God's kingdom on earth. The Messianic kingdom was to bring man's history to its fulfillment here on this earth created by God for that purpose.

The New Testament belongs to the same tradition of belief. This is the significance of another strange doctrine, prominent in the New Testament, the promise of the Second Coming of Christ. Why should Christ return to this earth, unless this earth is to be the locale of God's Kingdom, the scene of the consummation of all things? " I saw a new heaven and a new earth " (Rev. 21:1), a renovated physical order — the whole earth, like man's " body," not annihilated but perfected. " I saw the holy city . . . coming down from God out of heaven " (Rev. 21:2). This doctrine is the cosmological counterpart of the doctrine of the resurrection of the " body." Just as the individual at the end will not escape from his body but will find it changed and glorified, so also the human race will not eventually soar away from this earth to heaven, but will find the whole physical order transfigured and transformed into the locale of God's glorious and everlasting Kingdom.[9]

There is no suggestion here of disembodied " souls " painfully making their way up to heaven, there to exist for all eternity as pure " spirits." Just the opposite: God comes down to man; the Word is made flesh; heaven comes down to earth; the holy city comes down from God out of heaven. " And I heard a great voice out of heaven saying, Behold, the tabernacle of God is with men, and he will dwell with them, and they shall be his people, and God himself shall be with them, and be their God (Rev. 21:3).

Thus, at the end of the Bible, in its doctrine of the last things, as at the beginning, in its doctrine of the first things, the eternal significance of the whole realm of the physical is unmistakably asserted. This is part of what William Temple meant when he wrote:

" It may be safely said that one ground for the hope of Christianity that it may make good its claim to be the true faith lies in the fact that it is *the most avowedly materialist* of all the great religions. It affords an expectation that it may be able to control the material precisely because it does not ignore or deny it, but roundly asserts alike the reality of matter and its subordination. Its own most central saying is, ' The Word was made flesh,' where the last term was no doubt chosen because of its specially materialistic associations. By the very nature of its central doctrine Christianity is committed to a belief in the ultimate significance of the historical process, and in the reality of matter and its place in the divine scheme." [10]

We may add that the implications of this Biblical materialism for the Biblical anthropology — implications that are underlined by the doctrine of the resurrection of the body as opposed to the " religious " doctrine of the immortality of the separated soul —

are as follows: first, the "body" is an essential aspect of human personality and not a detachable part eventually to be cast aside; and, secondly, the whole person, and not a disembodied "soul," is destined for eternal life.

MAN AS AN "ANIMATED BODY"

This brings us to the more particular question as to whether there is in the Bible any trace of body-soul dualism. We shall have to leave an examination of the New Testament position for a separate chapter. We will begin here with a consideration of the Old Testament view.

The definitive work on this question has been done by H. Wheeler Robinson.[11] He amassed overwhelming evidence to prove that there is little or no trace of body-soul dualism in the Old Testament. "The Hebrew idea of personality is *an animated body and not [as in Greek thought] an incarnated soul*."[12] As for the word *nephesh,* translated "soul" in our English versions, either it means the personal pronoun, the self, the whole man, and has no reference to the inner as opposed to the outer life, or it means the principle of life, breath or breath-life, and is quasi-physically conceived.[13] In either case a falsely "spiritual" tone is given when *nephesh* is translated "soul." Approaching the question from the other side and asking what the Hebrews had to say about the "body," we arrive at the same conclusion. We find, in fact, that in the Hebrew language there is no distinct word at all for "body." The Hebrews did not need one, because they did not separate the "body" from the "soul." In Wheeler Robinson's words:

"Hebrew has no proper word for body; it never needed one so long as the body was the man; definition and nomenclature come only when there is some conscious antithesis. The antithesis is not reached in the Old Testament, nor could it be reached along native lines of Hebrew thought."[14]

And again elsewhere he says:

"The idea of human nature [in the Old Testament] implies a unity, not a dualism. There is no contrast between the body and the soul, such as the terms instinctively suggest to us." [15]

The same authority also pointed out that just as *nephesh* is thought of in quasi-physical terms, so in the Old Testament the bodily organs are regarded as performing psychical functions. Thus the heart thinks, the kidneys emote, the bowels feel sympathy, the eye sees, and the ear hears. Physical organs are centers of psychical activities. In short, the Hebrews, though ignorant of the actual physiological nervous system and brain, nevertheless in their own way recognized the dependence of psychical activities on the physical organism. The difference is that what modern science centralizes in the brain and nervous system they distributed throughout all the bodily organs.[16] But the Old Testament shares with modern science the same essential idea, namely, the interrelatedness and inseparability of the "body" and the "soul." "As the Hebrew myth and legend often enshrine permanent truths about God, so the Hebrew idea about man seems to have anticipated by intuition some of our modern science." [17]

It may be thought that we are here reading too much into what some would regard as just the "primitive materialism" of the ancient Hebrews. It might be pointed out that something of the same kind can be found in the "materialism" of the early Milesian philosophers of Greece, and elsewhere. The Greeks, however, it might be said, soon went beyond this primitive stage of thought and developed the "higher" concept of pure spirit or mind.

There is doubtless some truth in this contention. But certain considerations about the development of thought in general are relevant here. Very often human thought develops dialectically through three stages. The second stage is an antithesis of the first, and rightly draws attention to certain aspects of the subject under discussion that the first had neglected. The third stage is a synthesis of the first two, and often, if not always, takes the form

of a "recapitulation," much richer and fuller, of the initial position. Applying this analysis to the history of anthropological
conceptions, we can call the first stage "primitive materialism,"
and the second "spiritual idealism." The third stage in this development would be represented by the kind of conception we have
advocated in the previous chapter. We might call this view of
man "neomaterialism," claiming that it does justice to all the
facts that gave rise to idealism and to the "religious" anthropology, without falling into their errors. On this interpretation,
the "materialism" of the Old Testament might well be called
an anticipation of the views of modern science. For the final
stage of this development is a recapitulation of the earliest on a
higher level.

Returning to our study of "body" and "soul" in the Old
Testament, we must now try to answer another question. If it
is true that "for the Hebrews, man is a unity and . . . a complex of parts, drawing their life and activity from a breath-soul,
which has no existence apart from the body," [18] then what was
the Hebrew view of life after death and the Hebrew conception
of man's ultimate destiny? We have already referred to the fact
that the Hebrews had no idea of the immortality of the soul in
the Greek sense. It is now obvious, from the analysis just given,
that it was impossible for them even to conceive of disembodied
human existence. Nevertheless, the dead were certainly supposed
to exist in some sense. This is clear from the episode of Saul
and the woman with the "familiar spirit," who brought up
Samuel (I Sam. 28:7 ff.). It is clear from this and other passages
that the "shades" of the dead were thought of as continuing
to exist in Sheol. But the point is that the word that the Old
Testament uses in this connection is always "shades" and never
"souls" or "spirits." [19] The significance of this usage is that, in
this view, what continues to exist is not a part of man, such as
his "soul"; existence in Sheol lacks both body and soul, and
therefore has no vitality at all. [20]

" Man's nature is a product of two factors — the breath-soul which is his principle of life, and the complex of physical organs which this animates. Separate them and man ceases to be, in any real sense of personality; nothing but a shade remains, which is neither body nor soul." [21]

What continues to exist in Sheol is simply a " faint replica " of what the personality was as a whole.[22]

This miserable kind of survival was not, of course, the center of the hope of Israel. This hope, as we have mentioned, was directed elsewhere, toward the realization of the Messianic expectations here on earth. This was partly because, for the ancient Hebrews, the ultimate unit was not the individual but the nation, and therefore the fulfillment for which they looked was a corporate fulfillment. It was only later, when the national hope waned, that we find any idea of an individual future life beyond the grave.[23] And when Hebrew thought eventually began to develop along these lines, it arrived, for obvious reasons, not at the idea of the immortality of the independent soul, but at the idea of the resurrection of the body. This doctrine is already found in germ in two Old Testament passages (Isa. 26:19; Dan. 12:2). It is significant that in both passages the idea is connected, not with some future life in a nonmaterial realm, but with the Messianic kingdom to be established here on earth — in fact, in Palestine, with Jerusalem as its center.[24]

It is true, as we have said, that the idea of the immortality of the soul in the Greek sense may be suggested in some passages in the wisdom literature and is definitely found in places in the Apocrypha. This line of thought was later developed in the Hellenistic Judaism of the Alexandrine School, in the inter-Testamental period, of which the religious philosopher Philo is the outstanding example. This Hellenistic Judaism may have had some influence on the New Testament writers and on the early Church Fathers. But it was Palestinian Judaism, carrying on the classical Hebrew tradition, that provided the chief Hebrew background of the New Testament. It led, among other things, to the characteristic New Testament eschatological idea of the resurrection of the body, and this notion was part of that complex of ideas that was " unto the Greeks foolishness."

We may summarize the findings of this chapter by repeating that both the Biblical attitude to the physical and the Old Testament view of man are quite contrary to the " religious " anthropology and are by no means inconsistent with the evidence collected by the modern sciences about the nature of man.

CHAPTER IX

"Body" and "Soul"
in the New Testament

IT WOULD BE VERY UNLIKELY that a library of books, such as the Bible is, written by many different people varying in gifts and living in widely separated periods of time, would be perfectly consistent and uniform in all its views. It is certainly the case that in the Bible we find traces of several different traditions and thought-systems. The remarkable fact, about which Biblical scholars are in increasing agreement, is that there is a very high degree of unity in the principal ideas that are developed throughout the books of the Bible.

In trying to ascertain the Biblical teaching on any particular subject, we should concentrate on the main direction and momentum in the development of the relevant ideas, disregarding the minor deviations and departures from the norm. This is what we have done in tracing the Old Testament understanding of man. We have recognized that there are some traces of the " religious " anthropolgy in the wisdom literature and especially in the Apocrypha, but we have maintained that these were unimportant accretions of Greek thought and that they did not represent the main Biblical tradition on this subject.

In the inter-Testamental period, these Greek ideas flourished more vigorously in certain Jewish circles, notably in the Hellenistic Judaism of Alexandria. This was the background of Philo's well-known attempt to work out a synthesis of Greek and Hebrew ideas. This kind of influence was undoubtedly strong at the time when the New Testament books were written. Not only were these books written in the Greek language, but their authors were also exposed to the Greek way of thinking, and a writer like the author of the Fourth Gospel may well have been a follower of Philo before he became a follower of Christ.

It would not be surprising, then, if some traces of the dualism and asceticism of the "religious" anthropology were to turn up in the Gospels and Epistles. It seems beyond question that they do. The following questions then arise. Are these Greek ideas in the New Testament, like their predecessors in the wisdom literature and the Apocrypha, to be considered as minor and alien intrusions in the main stream of thought? If so, then we have to reconstruct the normal New Testament view of man, disregarding these unimportant remainders of a quite different and inconsistent anthropology. Or are we forced to come to the conclusion that already in the New Testament itself, and even earlier, there existed a synthesis of Greek and Hebrew ideas and that this synthesis is the appropriate human vehicle for the communication of the gospel? If this is the case, then the patristic and medieval anthropologies, where they incorporate Greek ideas, do not represent a departure from the Biblical teaching but are simply a development of it.

It should be apparent by now that we shall adopt the former alternative. It will be our contention that the main line of thought in the New Testament view of man, as in the Old Testament, is radically different from, and irreconcilable with, the "religious" anthropology. It is the Hebrew, and not the Greek, conception that the New Testament, for the most part, assumes.

THE FIRST THREE GOSPELS

In order to establish this contention, we shall turn first of all to the Synoptic Gospels and the sayings ascribed there to our Lord himself. Here we must guard against the tendency to assume that the Greek words in which these sayings are expressed must be interpreted in a Greek way. Our Lord spoke Aramaic and not Greek, and the meaning of his words and phrases must be sought, not in the Greek, but in the Hebrew background out of which, humanly speaking, he sprang.

This observation is relevant, first of all, to the use of the words "soul" and "body and soul" in the dominical sayings. In Hebrew thought, as we have seen, the word translated "soul" regularly stands simply for the personal pronoun and means the self. And the phrase "body and soul," though its occurrence is rare in both Testaments, stands for the Hebrew idea that man is an "animated body" and not for the Greek view that he is an "incarnated soul."

It is in this way that we must understand the verse: "And fear not them which kill the body, but are not able to kill the soul; but rather fear him which is able to destroy both soul and body in hell" (Matt. 10:28). This saying is always cited by those who believe that the New Testament, and indeed Jesus himself, asserts the essential immortality and incorruptibility of the soul, with all the dualistic implications of this belief. Thus Dr. Eugene Fairweather, in drawing attention to this passage, writes that here "the doctrine of the immortality of the soul, subject only to divine omnipotence, is plainly indicated." [1] But it is only "plainly indicated" if the verse is interpreted in terms of Greek presuppositions. And there is no reason for supposing that Jesus thought in such terms. The Judaism in which he was brought up was Palestinian and not Hellenistic. If we interpret this passage in the light of its Hebrew background, the plain meaning seems to be this: "Fear not man who can only bring your present existence to an end but cannot annihilate the essential self; but fear God who is able to destroy the whole man eternally." [2]

There are only a few other passages in the Synoptic Gospels that might be taken to imply a Greeklike depreciation of the bodily and earthy, on the one hand, and an exaltation of the "spiritual" and heavenly, on the other, along with the body-soul dualism that such a contrast implies. We may cite the following:

"Lay not up for yourselves treasures upon earth, where moth and rust doth corrupt, and where thieves break through and steal: But lay up for yourselves treasures in heaven, where neither moth nor rust doth corrupt, and where thieves do not break through nor steal" (Matt. 6:19, 20).

"Take no thought for your life, what ye shall eat, or what ye shall drink; nor yet for your body, what ye shall put on. Is not the life more than meat, and the body than raiment? . . . Therefore, take no thought, saying, What shall we eat? or, What shall we drink? or, Wherewithal shall we be clothed? . . . for your heavenly Father knoweth that ye have need of all these things. But seek ye first the kingdom of God, and his righteousness; and all these things shall be added unto you" (Matt. 6:25 ff.).

We should notice, first of all, that the importance of the body and of physical needs in general is by no means denied here. The body and its needs are far from being depreciated. "Is not the life more than meat, and the body than raiment?" Man's physical existence is *more* than a question of food and clothes; it has a higher significance and destiny. Moreover, "your heavenly Father knoweth that ye have need of all these things" and "all these things shall be added unto you." There is not the slightest suggestion here of any "puritanical" suppression of the physical demands; it is simply a question, as everyone except the most extreme advocates of free self-expression would agree, of subordinating the physical requirements and putting them in their proper place. It is a question of putting first things first. But this does not mean that second things are denied any place at all. Far from it; in their proper place they receive their proper satisfaction. "Seek ye first the kingdom of God . . . and all these things shall be added unto you."

"The kingdom of God" in the one passage and the "treasures in heaven" in the other stand for the true end of life; they symbolize God's ultimate purpose for man. This end and purpose should be our primary aim, the final good in accordance with which we should make our decisions. Food, drink, clothing,

" treasures on earth " have their place and value, but only in relation to this highest value. And this ultimate end is the Kingdom of Heaven established on earth. It is the transfiguration (not the annihilation) of the whole physical order and of everything in it.

THE JOHANNINE LITERATURE

We turn next to the Gospel and Epistles ascribed traditionally to Saint John. In this body of writing we seem, at first sight, to come upon a definite strain of hostility to the world and the flesh, very similar to the attitude of the " religious " anthropology. The following are representative passages:

" That which is born of the flesh is flesh; and that which is born of the Spirit is spirit " (John 3:6).

" It is the Spirit that quickeneth; the flesh profiteth nothing " (John 6:63).

" He that hateth his life in this world shall keep it unto life eternal " (John 12:25).

" In the world ye shall have tribulation: but be of good cheer; I have overcome the world " (John 16:33).

" Love not the world, neither the things that are in the world. If any man love the world, the love of the Father is not in him. For all that is in the world, the lust of the flesh, and the lust of the eyes, and the pride of life, is not of the Father, but is of the world. And the world passeth away, and the lust thereof: but he that doeth the will of God abideth for ever" (I John 2:15–17).

All this sounds very like that Greek and Eastern denigration of this world that condemns it as ephemeral and bad in contrast to the purity and eternity of the " spiritual " realm. Indeed, the Greek doctrine of immortality, always part of such a view, seems clearly indicated in the last sentence quoted, as well as in the words, " Whosoever liveth and believeth in me shall never die " (John 11:26; cf. ch. 6:50–58).

In considering such passages, we must remember, first of all, that in the Johannine literature and, for that matter, in the Bible generally, there is an ambivalent attitude to the world and the flesh. On the one hand, as created by God, they are evaluated as inherently good. Indeed, it is in The Gospel According to St. John itself that we read that " God so loved the world, that he gave his only begotten Son " and that " God sent not his Son into the world to condemn the world; but that the world through him might be saved " (John 3:16–17). The world, as made by God, is good, and he loves it with an everlasting and unfailing love. On the other hand, according to the Bible, this world has fallen away from its Creator. It is a " fallen " world and is in rebellion against God. It is in its " fallen " and rebellious condition that the world is opposed by God and should be resisted by man. The fact that it is " fallen " does not mean, however, that God will destroy it. The New Testament teaching is that he has taken decisive steps to re-create and save it.

Similarly, the flesh as made by God is good — so much so that it is possible, as Saint John again tells us, for the Word of God to *be made flesh*. But the flesh too is " fallen " and has become bad. However, it will not for that reason be annihilated by God. On the contrary, the Word was made flesh in order to remake and to redeem our flesh. Thus, Christians are called, not to leave the flesh and the world and depart to some other realm, but rather to remain in the flesh and in the world. " I pray not that thou shouldst take them out of the world " (John 17:15). " Now I am no more in the world, but these are in the world " (John 17:11). " As thou hast sent me into the world, even so have I also sent them into the world " (John 17:18). Christians must remain in the world; it is in itself good and it is their abode. On the other hand, " they are not of the world, even as I am not of the world " (John 17:16). They are not " worldly," in the sense of acquiescing in the world's " fallen " condition. Because of the ambivalent status of the world, as both created by God and " fallen," Chris-

tians are in an ambivalent relation to the world: they are in, but
not of, the world. What exactly it means to be "of the world,"
to be worldly and fleshly-minded, and what is meant by the contrast between "the world" and "the flesh," on the one hand, and
"the Spirit," on the other, are questions that we shall leave until
we come to the Pauline material that deals at length with this
subject.

We have still to deal with the Johannine passages that state,
in the English version, that whoever believes in Christ will abide
forever or "never die." If such a person never dies, then it follows, since the body is certainly doomed to dissolution, that there
is a part of man that is at any rate capable of immortality. And
if this is the case we have arrived again at dualism. Once more,
however, a quite different interpretation is possible, especially
if we look at the Greek original. First of all, in the Greek, the
adjective in phrases such as "everlasting life" and "eternal life"
is *aiōnios*. Now the noun *aiōn* in the New Testament very often
means "the age to come"; and therefore the adjective *aiōnios*
may very well mean, not "everlasting," in the sense of continuous,
unbroken survival, but rather "having to do with the age to
come." If this is the case, then "eternal" life means the kind of
life that belongs to the age to come; and "everlasting" is a mis-
translation.

In the same way, if we look at the Greek of the verses translated, "Whosoever liveth and believeth in me shall never die"
(John 11:26), and, "He that doeth the will of God abideth for
ever" (I John 2:17), we shall find that in both cases the relevant
verses might be translated literally, "Will not be dead," or, "Will
abide in the age to come." This interpretation seems to be confirmed by two other passages in which the believer is promised
eternal or *aiōnios* life:

"And this is the will of him that sent me, that every one which
seeth the Son, and believeth on him, may have everlasting [*aiōnios*]
life: and I will raise him up at the last day" (John 6:40).

"Whoso eateth my flesh, and drinketh my blood, hath eternal [*aiōnios*] life; and I will raise him up at the last day" (John 6:54).

The meaning here seems unmistakable: The believer has *aiōnios* life, that is to say, "I will raise him up at the last day." Similarly, it should be noted that the saying translated, "Whosoever liveth and believeth in me shall never die," is given in the context of the raising of Lazarus from the dead, and immediately follows the great declaration, "I am the resurrection, and the life: he that believeth in me, though he were dead, yet shall he live" (John 11:25). In other words, in every case, *aiōnios* life is related, not to the immortality of the soul, but to the resurrection of the body at "the last day." It is an eschatological concept, developed from the Hebrew tradition, and not a metaphysical concept, borrowed from the Greek.[3]

There is one more point to be made in this connection. The Johannine teaching usually refers to eternal or *aiōnios* life as a present possession. The believer *has* eternal life here and now. How can this be so, if eternal life is the life proper to the age *to come?* The answer is that eschatological concepts like "the age to come" and "the last day" do not refer to the historical future; they are not temporal concepts at all; it is only the poverty of our language and thought-forms that makes it necessary for us to express them in this misleading way. The new Testament teaching is that in Jesus Christ the "last things" have broken into time and space and that the believer, in so far as he is "in Christ," has within himself a pledge and earnest of the final consummation.

Perhaps we have here too a clue to the persistent question: If the Christian view of the "future life" is entirely eschatological and has nothing to do with any "immortality of the soul," then what happens to the individual between the time of his death and the "time" of the general resurrection at the "last day"? The answer is that the question is asked in the wrong way; phrases like the "future life" and the "time" of the general

resurrection indicate that the problem is a pseudo problem, based
on a misreading of eschatological language in temporal terms.
There is no interval between the death of the individual and the
" last day " that has to be accounted for by postulating an intermediate state and a ghostly, disembodied survival. The " last
day " is not a future event; it is not an event in time at all. There
is therefore no " time " of the general resurrection, no " interval "
between the individual's death and the " last day," nor is it proper
to speak of eternal or *aiōnios* life as a " future " life.

This is a negative answer to a very pressing question. But the
truth is that the Bible tells us very little about what happens
" after " death or about the nature of the final consummation of
God's purposes for man. It may be that we are told as much as
we are capable of understanding. And that is certainly not very
much. Where we do not know the answers, it is best to say so,
and to remain frankly agnostic.

The Pauline Epistles

In Saint Paul we find a further doctrinal development of the
implications of the gospel. It seems probable that, as far as his
Jewish background was concerned, he was influenced by both
the Hellenistic and the Palestinian types of Judaism. He certainly
had some familiarity with Greek thought, and there are undoubtedly traces, here and there, of the " religious " anthropology
in his writings. We shall argue, however, that this influence is not
nearly so strong as is often supposed and that the main line of
his thought is a development of Hebrew ideas.

J. A. T. Robinson, in a most careful and thorough study of the
Pauline literature, asserts without hesitation that Paul's view of
man is derived from Hebrew rather than from Greek sources.[4]
For Greek thought, man is a soul incarcerated in a physical
frame, from which he hopes to escape. For the Hebrews and for
Paul, on the contrary, man is, in Wheeler Robinson's phrase, " an
animated body." In the words of Pedersen, " the body is the soul

in its outward form." [5] According to J. A. T. Robinson, Paul follows the Hebrew tradition as formulated in the dictum: " Man does not have a body; he is a body." " He is flesh-animated-by-soul, the whole conceived as a psychophysical unity." [6] In fact, in Paul's usage, as we shall see, the Greek word *sōma* (body) is very nearly what we mean by personality: it stands for the whole man. We remember again Wheeler Robinson's remark that for the Hebrews " the body was the man." [7] All this, of course, is almost the exact opposite of the Greek view.

If these were Paul's presuppositions, it follows that he could not possibly have adopted any form of body-soul dualism. The doctrine of the immortality of a disembodied soul would be just inconceivable. And it would be equally out of the question to identity the " body " and its appetites as the source of evil.

What are we to say, then, of the well-known Pauline contrast between the " flesh " and the " Spirit "? Let us look at two typical passages:

" For they that are after the flesh do mind the things of the flesh; but they that are after the Spirit, the things of the Spirit. For to be carnally minded is death; but to be spiritually minded is life and peace. Because the carnal mind is enmity against God: . . . So then they that are in the flesh cannot please God. But ye are not in the flesh, but in the Spirit . . . And if Christ be in you, the body is dead because of sin; but the Spirit is life because of righteousness. . . . Therefore, brethren, we are debtors, not to the flesh, to live after the flesh. For if ye live after the flesh, ye shall die: but if ye through the Spirit do mortify the deeds of the body, ye shall live " (Rom. 8:5 ff.).

" This I say then, Walk in the Spirit, and ye shall not fulfil the lust of the flesh. For the flesh lusteth against the Spirit, and the Spirit against the flesh: and these are contrary the one to the other . . . And they that are Christ's have crucified the flesh with the affections and lusts. If we live in the Spirit, let us also walk in the Spirit " (Gal. 5:16 ff.).

These two passages are always cited to support the charge that Christianity, especially in the Pauline version, was responsible for spreading the doctrines of dualism, antiphysical asceticism, and " spiritual " otherworldliness in the Western world.[8]

The first thing to point out, in showing that such an interpretation of the Pauline teaching is entirely mistaken, is that Paul in these and similar passages never uses the Greek words for " body " and " soul " (*sōma* and *psychē*). He always employs a different pair of terms, namely, *sarx* and *pneuma* (translated " flesh " and " spirit "). If he had intended to take over the typical Greek body-soul dualism, he would certainly have used the Greek words *sōma* and *psychē* that were standard in that doctrine. But his antithesis is, in fact, an entirely different one, and he therefore uses a quite different set of words in which to express it.

What really clinches the argument against the dualistic and " puritanical " interpretation of the Pauline contrast is the list of " lusts " or " works of the flesh " that he gives in one of the very passages cited (Gal., ch. 5). There are seventeen " works of the flesh " listed there, and only six of them have any connection with the " body," as usually understood: " adultery, fornication, uncleanness, lasciviousness, drunkenness, revellings, and such like." And, of course, it is obvious that what is referred to here is the abuse of physical appetites and not the appetites themselves. But what is far more telling is that the remaining eleven " lusts " have nothing whatever to do with physical impulses and desires. The other " works of the flesh " are " idolatry, witchcraft, hatred, variance, emulations, wrath, strife, seditions, heresies, envyings, murders." In another place, Paul writes, " Ye are yet carnal: for . . . there is among you envying, and strife, and divisions " (I Cor. 3:3). This is what it means to be " carnal " and " fleshly-minded "; this is what it means to be " worldly," and to " live after the flesh." These are " the affections and lusts " of the flesh.

This seems to prove conclusively that in Paul the phrase " the flesh " does not stand for one part of man, such as his " body," nor the phrase " the Spirit " for another part, such as his " soul," the former being thought of as by nature bad and the latter good.

At the same time, Paul is certainly making a very sharp antithesis between " the flesh " and " the Spirit." What do these terms stand for, and what is the nature of the contrast that he has in mind? There can be no doubt that " the flesh " and " the Spirit " stand, not for two separate and opposing parts of human nature, but rather for two different kinds of man.   ,

The word *sarx* (flesh) in the Pauline epistles frequently means just the whole man, regarded from one point of view.[9] In this, Paul is following a fairly common Biblical usage. We recall sayings like " all flesh is grass," " all flesh shall see the salvation of God," and " the Word was made flesh." So in Paul, *sarx* is often [10] interchangeable with the personal pronoun. And the point of view from which the whole man is here regarded is the point of view of his creatureliness, his oneness with nature, and " his difference and distance from God "[11]; here *sarx* stands for the " natural man." In some cases, *sarx* means no more than this, and therefore has no sinful connotations at all.

More frequently, however, and especially in the passages where " the flesh " is contrasted with " the Spirit," *sarx* stands for the whole man, not only in his natural status, but in his " fallen " and unregenerate nature, in the same way that the " natural man " in Christian theology usually means sinful man. In this usage, *sarx* means the whole man regarded from the point of view of his sinfulness. But this sinfulness does not reside in the physical aspects of his nature in contrast to the alleged purity of his " spiritual " dimension. Man's sinfulness, according to the Pauline (and indeed the whole Biblical) teaching, consists precisely in his refusal to admit his creaturely status and in his unwillingness to recognize his " difference from God." Instead of recognizing that he is a creature of God, he wants to " set up on his own "; he claims absolute autonomy and complete self-sufficiency.

This is how J. A. T. Robinson, giving a long list of references, summarizes the Pauline position on this question:

"Living 'after the flesh' is sinful not because the flesh is evil or impure but because such an attitude is a denial of the human situation over against God . . . a distortion of the fundamental relation of the creature to God. One could describe the situation by saying that *sarx* as neutral [the first meaning quoted above] is man living in the world, *sarx* as sinful [second meaning] is man living for the world; he becomes 'a man of the world' by allowing his being-in-the-world, itself God-given, to govern his whole life and conduct. . . . Consequently, as Bultmann rightly stresses, 'the mind of the flesh' stands primarily for a denial of man's dependence on God and for a trust in what is of human effort and origin." [12]

Thus, as Robinson goes on to point out, the passage beginning, "Having begun in the Spirit, are ye now made perfect by the flesh?" (Gal. 3:3) refers "not to a lapse into sensuality but to a return to reliance upon the law and represents human self-sufficiency." Similarly "fleshly wisdom" (II Cor. 1:12) is "a man's trust in his own knowledge and experience" rather than in God. Thus Paul "recapitulates the message of the Old Testament: 'Cursed be the man that trusteth in man, and maketh flesh his arm, and whose heart departeth from the Lord'" (Jer. 17:5). *Sarx,* in this usage, is man with his whole nature corrupted by the sin of titanic pride; it is the condition of man who, being an adjective, claims to be a noun.

Thus, the meaning of "the flesh," like the meaning of "the world," is ambivalent in Paul, as in the Bible generally. The flesh and the world, as created by God, are man's intended lot and, as such, are the objects of God's love. But when the world and the flesh deny their creaturely status, rebel against God and claim independence and sufficiency, they become bad; and in this sense worldliness and carnal- or fleshly-mindedness are synonymous with sinfulness. But this view of sin has nothing in common with the antiphysical bias.

It is also obvious that the antithesis between "the flesh" and "the Spirit" has nothing in common with body-soul dualism. "The flesh" does not stand for one part of man, his "body," which is bad. " The flesh " stands, rather, for a certain kind of man. It stands for the kind of man in whom the whole person (the spiritual and psychical aspects, just as much as the physical, to revert to our earlier usage) is misdirected, because turned in upon himself in self-centeredness and self-satisfaction. In traditional theological language, " the flesh " stands for " fallen," sinful, unregenerate man.

If this is the case, the meaning of " the Spirit " in Paul is clear. " The Spirit " represents, not another part of man, his " soul," which is pure, but rather another kind of man. It represents the kind of man in whom the whole person (the physical and psychical, just as much as the spiritual aspects) is directed outward in love toward God and his neighbor; it is the man in whom we see " the fruit of the Spirit " — " love, joy, peace, long-suffering, gentleness, goodness, faith, meekness, temperance " (Gal. 5:22, 23). In short, it is redeemed man, the man who is " in Christ."

There is no actual man, of course, except Jesus Christ himself, who fully exemplifies what Paul means by " the Spirit " or the " spiritually-minded," in contrast to " the flesh " and the " fleshly-minded." In all men, even the best of them, a conflict continues: " For the good that I would, I do not: but the evil that I would not, that I do. . . . So then with the mind I myself serve the law of God; but with the flesh the law of sin " (Rom. 7:19–25). But this is not a conflict between the bad body and the pure mind. The conflict consists in the fact that in me, " the flesh," the old, self-centered man, is not wholly " crucified with Christ " but keeps rearing up to misdirect, not just my " body " and its appetites, but my whole being, in opposition to " the Spirit," the new man " in Christ," who is struggling to be born, " to rise with him." The Christian life involves a real and terrible conflict, but this conflict has no dualistic or " puritanical " implications.

So much for the meaning of *sarx* and *pneuma* in Paul. What, then, is the meaning of *sōma* and *psyche* in his writings? We have already mentioned Robinson's view that in Paul *sōma*

("body") is used much the same way as we use "personality":
"*sōma,* again like *sarx,* does not mean simply something external to a man himself, something he *has.* It *is* what he is. Indeed,
sōma is the nearest equivalent to our word 'personality.'" [13] Now,
in the Hebrew, it is *nephesh* that stands for the personal pronoun,
and Paul usually translates this word as *psychē.* Thus we arrive
at the conclusion that in Paul *sōma* and *psychē,* as well as *sarx*
and *pneuma,* are all used to stand for the whole man, but for the
whole man regarded from different points of view. [14]

Robinson distinguishes many different usages of the word
sōma in the Pauline writings. In all of them the term stands for
the whole, and not a detachable part of, man. Two of these usages
are relevant to our purpose. In the first meaning of *sōma,* it is
virtually equivalent to *sarx* and stands, like *sarx,* for the whole
man as seen in both his weakness and sinfulness, over against the
power and holiness of God. [15] Thus, in one passage, "the deeds
of the body," which must be "mortified," are none other than the
results of living "after the flesh" (Rom. 8:13). In fact, as Robinson observes, in some manuscripts they have become "the deeds
of the flesh." [16] "The identification of *sōma* with *sarx* seems complete. In fact, in Col. 2:11, it is closed in the phrase, 'the body
of the flesh' — the whole personality organized for, and geared
into, rebellion against God." [17] There is no question but that here
sōma stands for the whole man in his "fallen," sinful condition.
But it is equally obvious that *sōma* in this context has nothing in
common with the *sōma* of the *sōma-sēma* doctrine in the "religious" anthropology.

As Robinson points out, "The very phrase ["the body of the
flesh"] indicates the possibility of a *sōma* that is not *tēs sarkos*
["of the flesh"]." [18] This brings us to the second Pauline usage of
sōma that we must mention. In this usage, *sōma* means the whole
man as destined for membership in God's Kingdom; it stands for
man as God meant him to be. Thus *sōma,* while it may become
identified with *sarx,* due to man's "fallen" condition, is by no

means identical with *sarx*.[19] For *sarx* is destined for death and destruction, but *sōma* is the carrier of man's resurrection. While *sarx* stands for man " as wholly perishable," *sōma* stands for man " as wholly destined for God." [20] " While *sarx* stands for man, in the solidarity of creation, in his distance from God, *sōma* stands for man, in the solidarity of creation, as made for God." [21] The body is " for the Lord; and the Lord for the body. And God hath both raised up the Lord, and will also raise up us by his own power " (I Cor. 6:13, 14).

Man, as *sarx,* cannot inherit the Kingdom of God (I Cor. 15:50), but man, as *sōma* (and only as *sōma*), can. The fact that the *sōma* is to be raised indicates, of course, that it too must first die; for the resurrection is the " resurrection of the dead " (I Cor. 15:21). So also the *sōma* to be raised will be a radically changed *sōma.* The radical change is emphasized in the *locus classicus* on this subject and is described there as a change from a " natural [*psychikon*] body " to a " spiritual [*pneumatikon*] body " (I Cor. 15:35 ff.), that is to say, a change from human personality in its weakness and sinfulness to human personality as God meant it to be. And yet, as we saw earlier, this change, however radical, does not involve a completely fresh start. The resurrection " body," or new man, is not new in the sense that it has no connection with the old. It is new in the sense that it is the old made new. As Robinson points out, it is " not a *nea* but a *kaine ktisis* " [22] (II Cor. 5:17); or, to put it into contemporary idiom, it is not a brand-new but a reconditioned model. In Paul's analogy, it is like the relationship between the seed and the full-grown plant (I Cor. 15:35 ff.); there is a great change, but it is a change that perfects and brings to maturity. And this change happens, perhaps partly through growth and development in the Christian life, but only finally and completely, " in a moment, in the twinkling of an eye, at the last trump: for the trumpet shall sound, and the dead shall be raised incorruptible, and we shall be changed " (I Cor. 15:52).

It seems safe to say that this brief review of the New Testament writings has established our main contention. The New Testament anthropology, where it takes over earlier views, is in the Hebrew rather than the Greek tradition. There is little trace of body-soul dualism; instead, man is regarded as a unity. This personal unity that is man can be called, as a whole, either *sōma* (body) or *psychē* (soul) or *sarx* (flesh) or *pneuma* (Spirit), depending on the point of view from which man is being considered. But the point is that none of these terms refers to a part of man; they all refer to the whole. It follows that if man is an indivisible unity, there is no detachable part of him that can survive death. The New Testament, therefore, does not teach a doctrine of the immortality of the separated soul. Instead, it promises a resurrection of the whole man (the *sōma*). Finally, in this context of ideas, there can be no " puritanical " depreciation of, and hostility to, the physical aspects of human existence, with its accompanying exaltation of pure " spirituality." [23] The physical, both in the individual and in reality in general, has its essential and eternal role to play in human life. Man's ultimate destiny belongs, not to the ethereal regions but to " the world to come " " the world without end." And in this " world to come," the individual will be a " new body " and this earth will be a " new earth." But this newness will be a *kaine* and not a *nea* creation.

APPENDIX TO CHAPTER IX: ANTIPHYSICAL ASCETICISM AND OTHER-WORLDLINESS IN THE NEW TESTAMENT

There are a few passages in the New Testament that suggest a hostile attitude to sex and even a tendency to regard the married state as a kind of concession to human frailty; e.g., Matt. 19: 12: " There be eunuchs, which have made themselves eunuchs for the kingdom of heaven's sake. He that is able to receive it, let him receive it "; and a few notorious remarks of Saint Paul, especially I Cor., ch. 7, beginning, " It is good for a man not to touch a woman," and containing the assertion that " it is better to marry than to burn."

The remark attributed to our Lord in The Gospel According to St. Matthew is not repeated in any other Gospel. If it is taken as a disparagement of marriage, it is entirely out of keeping with our Lord's usual attitude to this state of life. If it is authentic, it may mean simply that some people are called to fulfill special roles in life that demand a sacrifice of some of the good things of life.

As for the various adverse comments on marriage that were made by Saint Paul, there are a number of possible explanations. It may be that we have here some traces of the antiphysical bias of the " religious " anthropology that simply cannot be reconciled with the over-all tenor of the normal Biblical view. Or these remarks may be " ad hoc recommendations to meet a specific local situation rather than general principles." Or they may be " due to the expectation that Christ would return at any moment " and that therefore no man should change his existing status. (See E. LaB. Cherbonnier, *Hardness of Heart* [Doubleday & Co., Inc., New York, 1955], pp. 83–84.)

There are also one or two passages in Saint Paul that suggest the possibility of escaping from the body in mystical vision, e.g., II Cor. 12:2, 3, and even the desire to escape from it altogether ultimately, e.g., ch. 5: 6–8. These again may be due to the influence of " religious " otherworldiness and, in that case, would certainly be inconsistent with Saint Paul's normal attitude to the " body " as outlined in this chapter. The inconsistency is apparent in the latter passage itself; for just before he speaks of being " willing to be absent from the body and present with the Lord," he writes (v.4), " We that are in this tabernacle do groan, being burdened: not for that we would be unclothed, but clothed upon, that mortality might be swallowed up of life." Here the doctrine of the resurrection of the body seems to be directly contrasted with the " religious " idea of the immortality of the " naked " soul (see v. 3).

In any case, as we have pointed out, and as Cherbonnier says, " The Bible contains within itself its own internal principles of self-criticism against which [such remarks] . . . can be tested." We have to bear in mind at all times " the spirit of the Bible as a whole " (*op. cit.,* p. 82). And " the spirit of the Bible as a whole " is definitely against the type of otherworldly mysticism that is suggested in the odd passage in Saint Paul.

CHAPTER X

The Nature and Destiny of Man

IN AN EARLIER CHAPTER [1] we attempted to show that it is possible to interpret the concepts of spirit and freedom without falling into the errors of either dualism and libertarianism on the one hand or one-level materialism and absolute determinism on the other. Our demonstration rested partly on pointing to certain facts that made the latter doctrines untenable and partly on making the important distinctions between subject and object and between causes and conditions. Without any reference to specifically Christian views we were led to the conclusion that man is a self-conscious psychosomatic organism, a conclusion that is entirely in keeping with the scientific evidence and at the same time enables us to do justice to the facts to which the "religious" anthropology bears a kind of mistaken witness.

Man is an organism in which matter is so organized that the resulting whole enjoys and suffers a peculiar type of consciousness, namely, self-consciousness. This self-consciousness enables him to be both rational and purposive and, to that extent, free. It is to this status of man as a whole that we refer when we speak of his "spirit." It is because he enjoys and suffers this status that he is not only a physical and sociopsychological unit but also a spiritual being, and not only an object, determined by impersonal forces, but also a subject exercising some degree of freedom. But when we refer to his capacity as a spiritual subject, we do not refer to some mystical part of his nature; we refer to the fact that man is a whole of a special kind.

In the last two chapters we have established the fact that the Biblical attitude to the physical is not only quite different from the " religious " anthropology but also entirely consistent both with the scientific evidence and with the anthropology that we ourselves have advocated. In what follows, both these central points will be amplified.

We must now proceed to delve farther into the Biblical view of man's nature and destiny in general. This view is given in three great Biblical doctrines: the doctrine of man's creation and " Fall " — aetiology; the doctrine of man's redemption — soteriology; and the doctrine of the " last things "— eschatology.

THE CREATION AND THE FALL OF MAN

The doctrine of the Creation and the Fall of man should be taken as one doctrine and not two. In the opening chapters of Genesis, there are, as we have noted, two different myths of creation, but this has nothing to do with the point we are making. What we are maintaining is that the story of creation and the Fall, in the form in which it appears in our Bible and in its theological significance, should be understood as one story, and not two. Further, this one story should not be interpreted as describing two events that are supposed to have happened one after the other in a time sequence. Instead, in our view, it calls attention, in dramatic fashion, to the two most fundamental facts about man, namely, that he is made in the image of God and that he is a sinner. It is one story, making two points.

This story, with its two main points, should not, of course, be taken as history or pseudo history, as philosophy or pseudo philosophy, much less as science or pseudo science. It tells us nothing about the natural and historical origins of man; but it tells us a great deal about his ultimate origin in God. It tells us nothing about biology or physiology; but it provides essential clues to the nature and meaning of human existence. It offers nothing in the way of philosophy or analytical psychology; but it is pregnant with the deepest insights into the tragedy and contradictions of human life.

Let us look at the story as it unfolds itself in the Bible:

" And God said, Let us make man in our image, after our likeness: and let them have dominion . . . over all the earth. . . . So God created man in his own image, in the image of God created he him. . . . And God saw every thing that he had made, and, behold, it was very good. . . . And the Lord God formed man of the dust of the ground, and breathed into his nostrils the breath of life; and man became a living soul.

" And the Lord God planted a garden eastward in Eden; and there he put the man whom he had formed. And out of the ground made the Lord God to grow every tree that is pleasant to the sight, and good for food; the tree of life also in the midst of the garden, and the tree of knowledge of good and evil. . . . And the Lord God commanded the man, saying, Of every tree of the garden thou mayest freely eat: But of the tree of the knowledge of good and evil, thou shalt not eat of it: for in the day that thou eatest thereof thou shalt surely die. . . .

" Now the serpent was more subtile than any beast of the field which the Lord God had made. And he said unto the woman, Yea, hath God said, Ye shall not eat of every tree of the garden? And the woman said . . . of the fruit of the tree which is in the midst of the garden, God hath said, Ye shall not eat of it, neither shall ye touch it, lest ye die. And the serpent said unto the woman, Ye shall not surely die: For God doth know that in the day ye eat thereof, then your eyes shall be opened, and ye shall be as gods, knowing good and evil. And when the woman saw that the tree was good for food, . . . and a tree to be desired to make one wise, she took of the fruit thereof, and did eat, and gave also unto her husband with her; and he did eat. And the eyes of them both were opened, and they knew that they were naked. . . .

" And the Lord God said, Behold, the man is become as one of us, to know good and evil: and now, lest he put forth his hand, and take also of the tree of life, and eat, and live for ever: Therefore the Lord God sent him forth from the garden of Eden. . . . So he drove out the man: and he placed at the east of the garden of Eden cherubim, and a flaming sword which turned every way, to keep the way of the tree of life " (Gen. 1:26, 27, 31; 2:7-9, 16, 17; 3:1-7, 22, 23).

The two main points in this story are, first, the making o͏͏͏
in the image of God — the creation of man; and, second, tʃ
ing of the forbidden fruit — the Fall of man. The fact thaᴛ ͏͏͏
two points are related in the story as though they were events
in a time sequence has led many to interpret the story as meaning that God first made man perfect and that then, subsequently,
man abused his gifts and fell into sin; thus we get the alleged
sequence of original events: perfection followed by the Fall, or
" original sin." There are insuperable objections, inherent in the
story itself, to this interpretation.

What are the God-given endowments, constituting the image
of God in man, as they come to light in this story? There seem
to be two: freedom and self-awareness. First, the command, " Of
the tree of the knowledge of good and evil, thou shalt not eat,"
obviously implies that they were free to obey or to disobey. Otherwise, the command has no point. Secondly, the comment, " They
knew that they were naked," clearly indicates that they had become aware of themselves, in a way that animals are not; they
had achieved self-consciousness. Now the main objection to interpreting the story as a history of events, in which perfection (the
image of God) is attained first and is then followed by the Fall,
is that in the story the gifts that constitute the image of God are
only fully realized in the eating of the forbidden fruit. For, in the
first place, real freedom is freedom to choose between good and
evil, and therefore involves the knowledge of good and evil. And
this knowledge is precisely the forbidden fruit. Thus we should
have to say that man becomes fully free and actualizes this aspect
of the image of God by disobeying God. " Behold," we are told
at the end of the story, after the Fall, " man is become as one of
us [like God] to know good and evil." Similarly, self-awareness,
the other aspect of the image, arises after and as a result of the
eating of the forbidden fruit: " The eyes of them both were
opened, and they knew that they were naked."

Thus, to interpret the story as a history of events in a time

sequence leads to the absurd conclusion that man became free
and self-conscious in and through an act of sin; in other words,
that man actualized the image of God by sinning against God.
There is clearly something very wrong with this kind of exegesis.

The mistake consists in trying to understand the story as a
description of events that are supposed to have happened one
after the other in time. Actually, the story is nothing of the kind.
It is, rather, an attempt to communicate the deepest truths about
man's contradictory nature. And these truths, like all profound
truth, are conveyed to us, not by means of a philosophical or scientific analysis, but in the telling of a story.

The long and often tragic history of the human race indicates
that man has godlike potentialities for knowledge and power,
and that he is always exercising these capacities in a way that can
be described only as demonic. The Genesis story, properly understood, throws light upon this basic contradiction. It tells us that
human nature is endowed with possibilities of genuine freedom
and self-awareness, but that in history self-awareness actually appears under the form of self-centeredness and free will under the
form of self-will. In William Temple's words, "As man arose
above subhuman forms of life, he found himself self-centered." [2]

There never was a time when man enjoyed a perfection of
freedom and self-awareness. Nor was there a time when he lost
these gifts and "fell" into sin. As soon as man emerged from
the animal level, he was already self-centered and self-willed.
This does not mean that historical man has no self-awareness and
no freedom. It means that he has a corrupt form of self-consciousness, namely self-centeredness, and a corrupt form of free will,
namely self-will. In so far as he has a form of self-consciousness
and freedom, he is capable of great achievements. In so far as he
is aware of himself as a subject, with the whole of nature over
against him as an object, he is able to acquire vast knowledge
and power in relation to nature, and indeed, as we have seen, in
relation to his social organization and psychical apparatus as well.

In so far as he possesses the capacity for conscious choice, a capacity that is enhanced by his increasing knowledge and power, he is able to rise to heights of moral achievement and to perform acts of genuine heroism, self-sacrifice, and love. These are all realities in human life. On the other hand, to the extent that his self-awareness and freedom are corrupt, these very achievements that are his glory are constantly being perverted, to his consternation and his shame. So that the more knowledgeable and powerful he becomes, because of his self-consciousness, the greater is the scope of his depredations, because of his self-centeredness. And the more righteous he becomes, because of his freedom, the more self-righteous he is apt to be, because of his self-will.

We interpret the Genesis story, then, in this way. As man evolved from the animal level, what was intended by God to develop into full self-awareness actually developed as corrupt self-awareness, namely self-centeredness. And what was intended by God to develop into real freedom actually developed as corrupt free will, namely self-will. The story of the creation and the Fall of man, then, is not to be considered as an account of two consecutive events that took place at the dawn of history. The idea of the creation of man in the image of God stands for the godlike potentialities of human nature. The idea of the Fall — most unfortunate misnomer — stands for the fact that man is always realizing these potentialities in a disastrously wrong way. These ideas, therefore, must never be separated as though they stood for two different events. The doctrine of the *imago Dei* does not teach that man ever possessed pure self-awareness, unmixed with self-centeredness, or pure freedom, uncontaminated by self-will. When one is reading the first two chapters of Genesis, one must not forget the third chapter. For they make up a single story and all belong together.[3] We may say that the image of God in man is God's purpose for man. In the striking words of Ryder Smith, the image of God describes not " what man was in the beginning, but what he is to be in the end "[4] — and what we believe he can be through Jesus Christ.

We are now in a position to relate the Genesis story and its teaching to our earlier conclusions about the meaning of the spirit and freedom of man.

The word " spirit," when applied to man, means that he is not just a psychosomatic organism but a self-conscious psychosomatic organism, not just a thing or object or part of nature, but also a person, a subject, and therefore in some measure transcendent over nature. In this explanation of the meaning of " the human spirit," it is clearly self-awareness, and not some part of, or substance in, man, that differentiates him from the rest of nature and makes it necessary in describing him to employ the category of the spiritual, as well as the category of the physical and socio-psychological. We know from our previous investigations that there is no tendency in the Bible to think of man as possessing a spiritual part or substance — a " soul "— in addition to his natural parts or "body." And we have just discovered that in the Genesis story, so important for an understanding of the Biblical view of man, it is a potential self-awareness that constitutes one aspect of the image of God in man. The image of God is man's potential spiritual status as a subject and a person. Man is potentially an " I," capable of achieving likeness to his Creator, whose great and mysterious name is, " I am that I am " (Ex. 3:14).

There is, however, another fact about the human spirit and one that is often missed by those who emphasize man's transcendence over nature and the possibilities of his knowledge and power.[5] The fact is that man's status as a person is terribly corrupted by sin. And sin is precisely the perversion of self-consciousness into self-centeredness. As such, it is something far more " original " and pervasive than fundamentalism and moralism ever understood. It is a disease that attacks the very roots of man's being. It is an infection that fouls his selfhood, his subjectivity, and his spirituality. This means that the knowledge and power that flow from his self-awareness are similarly perverted and never have the purely beneficial results that the optimists expect.

When we turn to the implications of the Genesis story for the meaning of human freedom, we shall have to go into somewhat greater detail. As we know, the scientific evidence, as to the extent to which the human individual is shaped by physical, social, and psychological forces, renders the libertarian conception of freedom, in terms of unrestricted power to choose, altogether untenable. On the other hand, the fact that man can come to know these forces undoubtedly gives him some degree of power and transcendence over them. We tried to recognize these various factors by distinguishing, first, between subject and object, and, second, between causes and conditions. As an object, man is conditioned by all the material factors that affect his nature; but as a subject, he is capable of freedom, in the sense that he is able to pursue deliberately chosen ends and is, to that extent, responsible for what he does and for what he becomes. Nevertheless, he always acts and develops within the limiting conditions of the material bases of life, and his freedom is always restricted in this way.

In examining the Biblical attitude to the physical and to the " body " and the " soul," we had no occasion to mention the Biblical attitude to freedom. We shall now find that it has little in common with the libertarian conception, and is therefore in no way undermined by the scientific evidence. We shall also find that the Biblical point of view, in this case, too, is consistent with the conclusions that we have previously reached.

First of all, the Bible insists that man is a creature. This means that his powers are finite and limited. There can be no such thing, in the context of the Biblical doctrine of creation, as unlimited human freedom. Man always has to act within the limits of his own created psychosomatic structure and of the created natural order in general. We have seen how the three sets of material factors — the physical, the sociological, and the psychological — provide three sets of limiting conditions from which the individual cannot escape. He cannot jump out of his own skin. These weighty and multitudinous forces restrict his freedom of choice, and they are inherent in the nature of man's existence. They constitute his creatureliness and his finitude. The libertarian conception of freedom ignores or denies this fact. But the Biblical view is not that man is free, in the libertarian sense. The Biblical teaching is that man is a creature and therefore subject to a vast variety of limitations. Making somewhat free use of Paul's phrase, "the elements of the world," and taking it to stand for the three sets of material factors, we may say that the Biblical conception, in direct opposition to the libertarian view, is that man is "in bondage under the elements of the world" (Gal. 4:3).

The implications of the Biblical doctrine of sin are even more fatal to the libertarian conception. The Genesis story of the Fall, as we have seen, does not refer to some alleged event that occurred at the dawn of human history. It refers rather to the fact that something is wrong at the roots of human nature. Sin is "original" in this sense, namely, that it is radical; it goes to the very roots of man's being. The source of evil is not to be found in one part of his nature — his "body" — while another part — his "soul" — remains pure and altogether transcendent over his "body." Evil is a deep-seated and pervasive corruption at the depths, and therefore affects all levels of man's being. Sin is a perversion of precisely the two potentialities that are the essence of personality, the capacity for self-awareness and the capacity for freedom. On these two capacities depend all man's intellectual, moral, and spiritual achievements. Without them, man could not become what he was meant to be — a full-grown person in the image of his Creator. But the possession of these potentialities carries with it the danger that they may be actualized in the wrong way. And this is what happens. Self-consciousness makes its appearance under the form of self-centeredness, and free will under the form of self-will. There is a deep corruption at the roots of human personality, a perversion in the depths of human subjectivity and spirituality. In man the old saying is terribly exemplified: "*Corruptio optimi pessima.*"

This interpretation of man's condition has an obvious bearing on the question of human freedom. In sin, interpreted as self-centeredness, the self is turned in upon itself in the worst and most ultimate kind of bondage — bondage to self. Self-love becomes the motive, and self-satisfaction the end, of all our thinking and our acting. And when the freedom that we have is employed in the interests of this misconceived " good," then it is abused and lost. Or, rather, real freedom has never been achieved.

We can see this process working itself out in various ways. First of all, in man's self-centered condition freedom to choose expresses itself in wrong choices. Repeated wrong choices harden into bad habits. And finally bad habits are solidified in permanent states of character, from which we are unable to shake loose; and our freedom of choice is lost. Secondly, repeated wrong choices eventually lead us into situations where the available choices are no longer between good and evil alternatives, but only between a greater and a lesser evil. And our freedom to choose between good and evil is lost. In the third place — and this is the worst feature of man's sinfulness — self-centeredness is a poison that fouls the springs of human action even in its aspirations after goodness. Every attempt that the self-centered self makes to overcome its self-love by acts of unselfishness and humility is apt to become fodder that feeds its pride. When I give up my seat to a woman on the bus, I congratulate myself on being unselfish. When I disclaim all credit for the act, I congratulate myself on being humble. Self-righteousness is the peculiar sin of " good " people. It is this that makes them so unattractive. We recall the child's prayer, " O God, make the bad people good, and make the good people nice." It is when " good " people become self-righteous that they cease to be " nice." It should be noted that the New Testament has some well-known strictures on this self-righteousness that is a form of bondage to self. As Berdyaev says,

" The typical Pharisee is the type of man in whom devotion to the law of goodness and purity, to an exalted idea, has been turned into . . . self-satisfaction . . . Man becomes a slave also to his higher nature . . . [He turns] the highest values into instruments of egocentric self-affirmation." [6]

When we remember that Freud called his superego man's higher nature and identified it as one source of compulsive behavior, we realize that here again the Biblical anthropology, far from being refuted, is actually confirmed by the findings of modern science.

There is more to be said on this point. Self-righteousness, the sin of " moral," law-abiding people, is usually accompanied by the claim that one's own ideas of what is right and good, true and beautiful (which are, in fact, largely conditioned by a host of irrational, material factors), have an absolute and eternal value, and that those who do not conform to them are willfully wrong-headed and wicked. Then finally, this kind of bondage to self, which insists on the universal validity of its own standards, often proceeds to impose its moral laws, as far as possible, on everyone, and especially on the younger generation. And it imposes them in an external and arbitrary fashion. This is the source of that repressive, legalistic morality to which our psychologists are rightly opposed. What is amazing is, not that they oppose it, but that they identify it with morality as such, and especially with Christian ethics. This reflects both their own ignorance and also the errors of much that passes for " Christian " teaching. For the New Testament is opposed, as strongly as modern psychotherapy, to this kind of morality. We have only to recall Jesus' attacks on the Pharisees, the representatives of legalistic morality, and Paul's repeated warnings against servitude to the " law," in order to realize that the morality in question is quite foreign to the New Testament ethics. Saint Thomas Aquinas was in the authentic Christian tradition when he suggested that the man who blindly obeys his passions is enslaved to the passions, while the man who represses his appetites through fear of the law is in bondage to the law and " acts slavishly." [7] There is agreement between the New Testament and modern psychology on the baneful effects of what Eric Fromm calls the " authoritarian " conscience and " authoritarian " ethics.[8]

Thus sin, as self-centeredness or bondage to self, involves the loss of freedom. If man, because of his creatureliness, is " in bondage under the elements of the world," he is also (which is much worse) in " the bondage of corruption " (Rom. 8:21) because of his sinfulness. Man's freedom is not only limited because of his finitude, but is largely lost because of his self-centeredness. Or, to speak more correctly, since self-consciousness and free will actually make their appearance as self-centeredness and self-will, man's true freedom has never been achieved. Again we see how remote from the libertarian conception, and how perfectly consistent with the scientific evidence, is the Biblical view. Man, as he is, is not free: he is in bondage.

The Redemption of Man

The story of creation and the Fall, considered as a unity, tells us, first, what man was meant to be — an image and a son of God, enjoying " the glorious liberty of the children of God," and, second, what man has actually become — a " fallen " creature and a sinner, enmeshed in a fearful bondage. The potentialities that were meant to emerge as full self-consciousness and real freedom actually developed as self-centeredness and self-will.

What man was meant to be remains God's purpose for him. In the Genesis story this purpose — man's true end and destiny — is represented by the Garden, with the tree of life in the midst of it. At the end of the story man is expelled from the Garden, and cherubims are set up with " a flaming sword which turned every way, to keep the way of the tree of life " (Gen. 3:24). This symbolism should be kept in mind as we proceed.

The Genesis story is only the beginning of the Biblical account of man. The account is taken up again in the New Testament, with the proclamation of man's redemption and fulfillment in Christ. When God's purpose for man was frustrated by the various types of human bondage, God sent his Son into the world to deliver man both from "bondage under the elements of the world" and from the "bondage of corruption." These are the two aspects of Christ's redemptive or liberating work.

The first kind of bondage is associated with the limitations inherent in man's finitude. But because of sin these limiting conditions of his created existence have been transformed into compulsive and determining forces. His self-consciousness, on which his knowledge and power depended, developed as self-centeredness; hence his ignorance and weakness were, for centuries, far greater than they were meant to be. And this ignorance and weakness involved him in servitude to his natural environment, to his social organization, and to his psychical apparatus. But this kind of servitude was far from God's purpose for man. In the creation story, God said, " Let them have dominion . . . over all the earth " (Gen. 1:26). Men were meant to be the masters, not the slaves, of the material conditions of their existence. Christ came to deliver us from this kind of servitude; it was part of his redemptive (liberating) work.

Now, man is, in fact, delivered from this form of bondage by the knowledge and power that the various sciences afford. Modern medicine can help us to overcome the disordered functioning of the physical brain, the nervous system, the glands, and so on. We are no longer completely at the mercy (the slaves) of our physical equipment. Similarly, the discovery of the part played in shaping human personality and behavior by the psychical mechanisms enables the modern psychiatrist to give therapeutic treatment in this area. We are no longer completely at the mercy, no longer the helpless slaves, of our psychical apparatus. And, finally, our increasing knowledge of the facts and laws of social life enables us to control and improve our social organization. We are no longer the mere victims and products of the social *status quo*. In all these ways scientific knowledge and power make us more free in relation to the limiting conditions of our creaturely condition. It is science that enhances our freedom of choice, releases us from this first kind of bondage, and makes us more capable of enjoying " dominion . . . over all the earth."

Is it fanciful to suppose that all this has happened, in the " scientific " age, within the purpose of God and as part of Christ's redemptive work? Is it not the case that the knowledge and power of modern science furnish us with real evidence that the Holy Spirit is indeed leading us into truth, giving us power and making us free? It was Christ himself who promised that " when he, the Spirit of truth, is come, he will guide you into all truth " (John 16:13), and that " ye shall know the truth, and the truth shall make you free " (John 8:32), and who also said, " Ye shall receive power, after that the Holy Spirit is come upon you " (Acts 1:8) — knowledge, power, and freedom. No doubt he meant considerably more than this, as we shall see; but surely he meant this too. Paul summed it up in this way: " God hath sent forth the Spirit of his Son . . . wherefore thou art no more a servant [in bondage], but a son [free]; and if a son, then an heir of God [enjoying dominion over all the earth]" (Gal. 4:6, 7).

However, real freedom is not merely enhanced freedom of choice; it is not even freedom of choice raised to the " nth " power. There is another kind of freedom that is even more important. This is the kind of freedom that Engels called " knowledge of necessity " — though he misconceived the nature of the " necessity " in question. Marxist Communism understands that this real freedom has to do with the knowledge of, and conformity to, the true end of life, but it misunderstands the nature of man's true end. The point, however, that libertarianism misses altogether, is that real freedom resides, not in endless, unrestricted and capricious choices, but in choosing the true end and in committing oneself to it. Libertarianism, because it identifies freedom with choice itself, is afraid of any commitment that would limit the range of choices for the future. If I am committed to the belief that " man's chief and highest end is to glorify God, and fully enjoy him forever," then I am thereby precluded from a whole great set of possible choices. On the other hand, if this is man's true end, then, in committing myself to it, I am fulfilling my nature. And it is here, in this authentic self-fulfillment, that real freedom resides. Or, as *The Book of Common Prayer* suggests, in His " service is perfect freedom."[9] This is the freedom of fulfillment, as distinguished from freedom of choice. It is the freedom of a being that has fully realized all the potentialities of his nature.

Authoritarianism, in all its forms, both ecclesiastical and secular, rightly grasps the importance of the end but wrongly belittles or ignores man's freedom of choice, and so attempts to impose on its adherents what it believes to be the true end. Libertarianism rightly understands the importance of freedom of choice, but in its preoccupation with this kind of freedom fails to raise the vital questions: Freedom to choose what? For what ends and purposes are we to use our freedom of choice? On the right answer to these questions depends the attainment of real freedom. If we were to use our freedom of choice to choose the true end of life, then we should be on the way to full freedom, to " the glorious liberty of the children of God." " Where the Spirit of the Lord is, there is liberty " (II Cor. 3:17. Cf. John 8:36).

Our tragedy is that achievement of this real freedom is rendered impossible by sin. Sin is the service of, and bondage to, self. It means that our freedom of choice is used, not to choose God and his service, but self and the misconceived interests of the self. And the more we use our free choice in the interests of self, the more we come into bondage to self, and the further we recede from the " glorious liberty " of His service. As William Temple said, we need to be delivered "from the freedom which is perfect bondage, to the bondage which is perfect freedom." [10] Libertarianism cannot understand this paradox, that "bondage" to God should turn out to be "perfect freedom." Yet it is one of the deepest of all truths. For in the service of God we become what we were meant to be, his sons by adoption and heirs of his Kingdom. When we are no longer enslaved to the physical appetites, when we no longer suppress these appetites from fear of the moral law, when we do God's will because that is what we *love* to do, then at last are we free. [11]

As long as we remain centered on self, we remain in bondage to self, and this is "the bondage of corruption." Freedom from "bondage under the elements of the world," conferred by modern scientific knowledge and power, enhances our freedom of choice and increases our dominion over the earth, but it will not help us at the crucial point. On the contrary, as we should easily recognize in the age of "The Bomb," all this increased knowledge, power, and freedom, when employed by self-centered man, will only hurry us on the faster to perdition.

In the last analysis, then, everything depends on our deliverance from "the bondage of corruption." We believe that this redemption too has been accomplished by God in Christ, and accomplished in the only possible way. Man's perfect self-centeredness can be overcome only by the perfect self-sacrifice of perfect love, perfectly and terribly set forth on Calvary. It is the cross that opens the way out of the bondage of self-will into "the glorious liberty of the children of God." It is the cross that leads us away from self and toward the "perfect man, unto the measure of the stature of the fulness of Christ" (Eph. 4:13). It is the cross that heals the mutilations and distortions of our sinful nature and points to the real self-fulfillment that is found only in the attainment of man's true end.

The Fulfillment of Man

The New Testament proclaims that the Kingdom of God on earth — God's purpose for this world — is already established in principle by Christ's redemptive work, but will have its perfect fruition only at "the last day." Similarly, the liberating and fulfilling of man's nature, the establishment of the image of God in man, is being carried on in us now through all the manifold agencies of the Holy Spirit, but will have its perfect consummation only at "the end." We know from bitter experience that as long as history endures, self-love ("the flesh") will be constantly thrusting up to vitiate even our best and highest achievements, as individuals, as nations, and as a race. It is only at "the last day" that the "new man" ("the Spirit"), which is "Christ in us," will be fully realized, when "we shall all be changed, in a moment, in the twinkling of an eye, at the last trump: for the trumpet shall sound, and the dead shall be raised incorruptible, and we shall be changed" (I Cor. 15:51, 52).

What shall we be changed into? We shall be changed into the image of Christ, who is himself the image of God. We shall become children of God by adoption, as he is the Son of God by nature. We shall all come to the "perfect man." We shall all be "conformed to the image of his Son" (Rom. 8:29), who is "the express image of his person" (Heb. 1:3). "We all, with open face beholding as in a glass the glory of the Lord, are changed into the same image from glory to glory, even as by the Spirit of the Lord" (II Cor. 3:18). "And where the Spirit of the Lord is, there is liberty" (II Cor. 3:17). The perfection and fullness of life that are in Christ constitute the real self-awareness that man was always intended to have. And this liberty that belongs to "the Spirit of the Lord" is the real freedom for which man was always destined. God's eternal purpose will be accomplished and man will become what he was meant to be, a real person in the image of God. Then man will be really "perfect," that is, entire, whole, integral, with all aspects of his being, the physical and the social and the psychological, brought to their completion in the wholeness of " the spirit." " I pray God," said Paul, " your whole spirit and soul and body be preserved blameless unto the coming of our Lord Jesus Christ " (I Thess. 5:23).

Thus we find the " image of God " appearing both at the beginning and at the end of the Biblical account of man. The connection is established by our view that the " image of God " describes " not what man was ' in the beginning ' but what he is to be in the end." And yet in a sense the image is there all the time, in so far as man has in his nature, from the start, the necessary potentialities — the capacities for self-awareness and for freedom. But these capacities are developed in the wrong way so that man becomes self-centered and self-willed. Nevertheless, he remains a person; knowledge, power, freedom, and moral achievement remain possible for him; indeed they exist to illuminate the pages of human history. At the same time, these human glories are never what they might be, but are always subtly perverted by man's self-love. But, according to the Christian faith, there was one human person who was the " express " image of God and who by his redemptive work overcomes sin and enables men to be " changed into the same image from glory to glory."

This interpretation of the doctrine of the image of God in man indicates that many of the problems traditionally surrounding this subject are unreal. Was the image of God totally effaced at the Fall? If so, is historical man entirely reduced to the level of the rest of nature, has he no genuine personality left, so that totalitarianism is right in its contempt for the individual human being? Or did some " relics " and " traces " of the image survive the Fall? Does " original sin " involve man's " total depravity," or is it merely a misdirection of the will, leaving the reason essentially intact? What is the relation between what David Cairns calls the Old Testament or universal image and the New Testament image or Christ? [12] These and many other problems are quickly resolved, if we interpret the story of the Creation and the Fall of man as a single story, indicating that God endowed man with the potentialities necessary for the achievement of full-grown personality, and that these potentialities from the beginning were actualized in the wrong way. This does not mean that man never becomes a person, differentiated in certain respects from the rest of nature. It means that he becomes a corrupt kind of person, a self-centered person. He is still transcendent over nature; he still achieves great intellectual and moral victories. But his transcendence and his achievements tend themselves to be perverted by self-love. To speak of " relics " and " traces " of the image, or to speculate that it is only the will that is infected while the reason remains intact, is to misunderstand the situation; similarly " total depravity " is a misleading expression. It is simply semantic confusion to suppose that " part " of the image " survives " the Fall or that the image " survives " in a " part " of human nature. The image is what man might have been, if he had developed in an unperverted way. But he did not so develop; the potentialities on which the actualization of the image depended, and which constitute the roots and essence of personality, were corrupted. Thus all aspects of man's being appeared in distorted form.

Finally, the relationship between the Old Testament or universal image and the New Testament image, who is Jesus Christ himself, becomes clear. The universal image is the image distorted by sin, while the New Testament image is the image as God meant it to be in all men. And through the redemptive work of Christ, overcoming sin, we can all be " conformed to the image of his Son " who is " the express image of his person."

Now, by way of recapitulation and conclusion, we can show how the Biblical anthropology incorporates the truths of both the " religious " and the " scientific " anthropologies, while purging them of their errors. The doctrines of these latter anthropologies may be listed in parallel columns, showing that for each doctrine on the one side there is corresponding doctrine, at the opposite extreme, on the other. The fact that these doctrines are all ex-

A. *The "Religious" Anthropology*	B. *The "Scientific" Anthropology*
1. Body-soul dualism	1. One-level materialism
2. Antiphysical asceticism and its absolutistic ethics	2. Free self-expression and its complete relativism
3. Libertarianism	3. Absolute determinism
4. Immortality of the soul	4. Finality of death

tremes indicates that they are all erroneous. Nevertheless, they all stand for important truths about man. Indeed, it is their anxiety to protect the truths in question that leads the champions of these views to their extreme conclusions.

The first point to be made, in recapitulation and conclusion, has to do with the New Testament insistence on the resurrection of the body, as the major emphasis in its teaching on man's ultimate destiny. This Biblical doctrine tells us that it is not a disembodied "soul" or "spirit" that is destined for eternal life, but the whole man — spirit, in our sense of the word. And the adjective "eternal" translates the New Testament *aiōnios*, which means "having to do with the age" or "world to come"; and not "having to do with some ethereal realm of 'pure spirit.'" The life in question is the life of the Kingdom, to be achieved in its fullness in the consummation of all things "at the end." In that consummation, the three sets of material conditions, so indispensable to human nature as it is — the physical, the social, and the psychological — will all receive their perfection; they are not accidental factors to be shuffled off at death, but rather essential aspects of man's personal being, with eternal significance for his ultimate destiny.

Man is, and will be, a unified psychosomatic organism. This is
the truth contained in the one-level materialism of the " scientific "
anthropology (B. 1.). But he is also a self-conscious psychosomatic
organism, a subject and a person with a spiritual status. This is
the truth that is meant to be preserved by the body-soul dualism
of the " religious " anthropology (A. 1.), with its insistence that
man is not just a part of nature.

In the second place, the Biblical teaching is that man, as he is,
remains in fact a sinner. This is the truth that is buried in the
moralism of the " religious " anthropology (A. 2.), with its preoccupation with sin, the nature of which it misconceives. At the
same time, while man is a sinner, he remains man, and is therefore capable of recognizing and pursuing real values. This is the
truth of the absolutistic ethics, though it prematurely identifies
its own standards as absolute. Because man, as sinner, is in
" bondage " under the elements of the world, his standards are, in
fact, largely imposed upon him by irrational social and psychological forces; and because he is in the " bondage " of corruption
(self-love), he is constantly tempted to claim an absolute status for
these relative norms. This is the truth of the complete relativism
and the validity of the attack on " morality," characteristic of the
" scientific " anthropology (B. 2.). Further, these two types of
bondage mean that man is never able, by his own efforts, to
achieve real freedom. And this is the truth of the absolute determinism of the " scientific " anthropology (B. 3.).

Thirdly, while man remains in fact a sinner and in bondage,
Christ has already, in principle, conquered sin and delivered him
from slavery. The risen Christ is himself the first-fruits, the pledge
and earnest of " what we shall be " (I John 3:2) — " a perfect
man, . . . the measure of the stature of the fulness " (Eph. 4:13).
The perfect man is the man in whom the image of God is fully
realized; he is man as God from the beginning meant him to be;
he is man enjoying real freedom and real self-fulfillment. This
" glorious liberty of the children of God " is something very dif-

ferent from the libertarian conception of freedom as unrestricted choice. It is the freedom of complete self-fulfillment; it is the freedom of a being who has attained his true end and, therefore, has become what he was meant to be. Nevertheless, this is the truth that lies hidden in the "religious" notion of the "free soul" (A. 3.). And the self-fulfillment of the perfect man is something very different from the free self-expression of the "scientific" anthropology; nevertheless it is the truth to which that view (B. 2.) obscurely points. This self-fulfillment is the fulfillment of self-awareness and, therefore, of the true self. It is the actualization of the image of God in man, making him a son of God and a member of his Kingdom.

Finally, the Kingdom of God, to be established on earth in all its glory at "the last day," is man's ultimate destiny. Death is not the last word. This is the truth to which the "religious" doctrine of the immortality of the soul (A. 4.) bears mistaken witness. But the "soul" does not survive the death of the "body." This is the truth of the denial of immortality in the "scientific" anthropology (B. 4.). It is the whole man, transformed into the image of God, who is destined for eternal life in the Kingdom.

It was pointed out earlier that at the end of the Genesis story of creation and the Fall, man was expelled from the Garden and a flaming sword was set up to keep him away from the tree of life. There the Garden and the tree of life are symbols of God's original and eternal purpose for man. Now, it is a striking fact that the Garden and the tree of life, so prominent at the beginning, do not reappear until the very end of the Bible. In the book of Revelation, having to do with the "last things," we come upon the Garden and the tree again. "To him that overcometh will I give to eat of the tree of life, which is in the midst of the paradise of God" (Rev. 2:7). And "paradise," of course, is just the Persian word for "garden." Again, in the very last chapter of the Bible, we read that "they may have right to the tree of life, and may enter in through the gates into the city" (Rev.

22:14). And the "city" is the Kingdom, "the holy city, new
Jerusalem [the Garden built up into the City], coming down
from God out of heaven" (Rev. 21:2).

In the Old Testament and in Genesis, the Garden with its tree
is the symbol of God's purpose in the beginning. In the New
Testament and in Revelation, the Kingdom with its city represents the consummation of that purpose at "the end."

In one sense, "the end," with the Garden re-established and
transformed into the City and the Kingdom, does not belong to
the future; in Christ, the City and the Kingdom have already
come down to earth; in the incarnation, in the redemptive work
and resurrection of our Lord, and in the sacraments of his Church,
the "last things" have broken into time and history. "The kingdom of heaven is at hand" (Matt. 4:17).[13] "The kingdom of
God is among you" (Luke 17:21).[14] "Lord, remember me when
thou comest into thy kingdom. And Jesus said unto him, Verily
I say unto thee, To-day shalt thou be with me in paradise" (the
Garden) (Luke 23:42, 43).

In another sense, "the end" is not yet, and we wait for it:

"For the earnest expectation of the creature [the whole creation]
waiteth for the manifestation of the sons of God. . . . Because the
creature itself also shall be delivered from the bondage of corruption
into the glorious liberty of the children of God. For we know that the
whole creation groaneth and travaileth in pain together until now.
And not only they but ourselves also, which have the firstfruits of the
Spirit, even we ourselves groan within ourselves, waiting for the adoption, to wit, the redemption of our body. For we are saved by hope"
(Rom. 8:19, 21–24).

We wait and hope for the day when the King who hung upon
the cross will come again in glory, and will say to all who truly
love and serve him, "Come, ye blessed of my Father, inherit
the kingdom prepared for you from the foundation of the world"
(Matt. 25:34).

Still, when all this has been said and all our investigations have been completed, man remains a mystery to himself. As Reinhold Niebuhr said in the first sentence of his greatest work, " Man has always been his own most vexing problem." [15]

" What is man, that thou art mindful of him? and the son of man, that thou visitest him? " (Ps. 8:4).

" Such knowledge is too wonderful for me; it is high, I cannot attain unto it. . . . I will praise thee; for I am fearfully and wonderfully made " (Ps. 139: 6, 14).

Notes

CHAPTER I. CHRISTIANITY AND SCIENTIFIC NATURALISM

[1] See D. J. B. Hawkins, *A Sketch of Mediaeval Philosophy*, Ch. IV. Sheed & Ward, New York, 1947.

[2] *Op. cit.*, p. 89.

[3] A. N. Whitehead, *Science and the Modern World*, Ch. I. Cambridge University Press, Cambridge, 1946.

[4] *Op. cit.*, p. 14.

[5] *Op. cit.*, p. 15.

[6] *Op. cit.*, pp. 15, 16.

[7] *Op. cit.*, p. 16.

[8] Michael Foster, "Christian Theology and Modern Science of Nature." *Mind*, Vols. XLIV, 176, and XLV, 177.

[9] John Baillie, *Natural Science and the Spiritual Life*, pp. 18 ff. Oxford University Press, London, 1951.

[10] Quoted by Baillie, *op. cit.*, p. 20.

[11] *Op. cit.*, p. 22.

[12] *Op. cit.*, p. 24.

[13] Quoted by Baillie, *op. cit.*, p. 30.

[14] *Loc. cit.* Cf. Michael Foster, "Some Reflections on Science and Religion," *The Christian News-Letter*, No. 299, pp. 5 ff.

[15] Cf. Foster, *op. cit.*, pp. 13 ff.

[16] W. Temple, *Nature, Man and God*, p. 478. Macmillan, London, 1935.

[17] This interpretation of the Christian attitude to the physical order is defended in Ch. VIII, below.

[18] C. S. Lewis, *Mere Christianity*, p. 51. Geoffrey Bles, London, 1952.

[19] George McLeod, *The Coracle*, p. 9. The Iona Community, Glasgow, 1947.

[20] My earlier book, *Scientism, Man, and Religion*, The Westminster Press, Philadelphia, 1952, attempted to analyze the perversion of science in scientism. The present book attempts to examine the corruption of Christianity in "religion."

[21] See Ch. II, below.

[22] See Ch. V, below.

[23] See Part III, below.

[24] See Ch. VI, below.

[25] J. V. L. Casserley, *The Retreat from Christianity in the Modern World*, p. 24. Longmans, Green, London, 1952. The passage he refers to in Hoyle is found in the latter's *The Nature of the Universe*, pp. 116 ff. Blackwell, Oxford, 1952.

[26] Cf. the prayer in the office of Compline, in which the clause occurs: " That when our bodies lie in the grave, our souls may dwell with thee." This kind of thing is common in popular Catholic devotions.

[27] From John Donne's poem: " The Anniversary." I owe this reference to my colleague and theological sparring partner, Dr. Eugene Fairweather.

[28] Part III, below, offers a detailed exegesis and examination of the relevant Biblical passages which furnish the grounds for the interpretation of the Biblical view of man of which a very brief summary is given here.

CHAPTER II. THE ORIGIN OF THE " RELIGIOUS " VIEW

[1] Mary E. White in her essay, " The Greek and Roman Contribution," in *The Heritage of Western Culture,* ed. R. C. Chalmers, pp. 19–21. The Ryerson Press, Toronto, 1952. Italics mine.

[2] *Op. cit.,* p. 23.

[3] The Pauline antithesis between " the flesh " and " the Spirit " has little if anything in common with the Greek antithesis between " the body " and " the soul." This question is discussed fully below in Ch. IX.

[4] Pausanias 8. 37. 5.

[5] *Meno,* 81b, c; *Laws,* 701c, 845 f.

[6] Described by W. K. C. Guthrie, *Orpheus and Greek Religion,* pp. 171 ff. Methuen & Co., Ltd., London, 1935.

[7] *Phaedo, Phaedrus, Republic, Georgias.*

[8] E. R. Dodds, *The Greeks and the Irrational,* p. 146. University of California Press, 1951.

[9] *Cratylus* 400b, c.

[10] *Georgias,* 492d. Cf. *Phaedo* 62a.

[11] Fr. 14. *Clement of Alex.,* Miscellanies iii. 17.

[12] See E. R. Dodds, *op. cit.,* p. 139.

[13] *Loc. cit.*

[14] Herod. II. 81. Italics mine.

[15] K. Freeman, *Ancilla to the Pre-Socratic Philosophers,* p. 19. Harvard University Press, Cambridge, Massachusetts, 1948.

[16] Sextus Empiricus, *Pyrrh. Hyp.* 3.230. V. Macchioro, in *Eraclito,* Bari, 1922, has attempted to interpret Heraclitus' whole philosophy as based on "Orphism." See W. K. C. Guthrie, *op. cit.,* pp. 224 ff.

[17] K. Freeman, *op. cit.,* pp. 64 ff.

[18] *Phaedo* 78b.

[19] *Timaeus* 87e.

[20] *Phaedo* 64c. Italics mine.

[21] *Op. cit.,* 78b. Italics mine.

[22] *Republic* X. 611. Italics mine.

[23] *Timaeus* 90a, c. Cf. 41d. Italics mine.

[24] The references that follow are cited by W. K. C. Guthrie, *op. cit.,* pp. 199 ff., and 232 ff.

[25] See Ch. IX, below.

[26] See Ch. III, below.

[27] *The Speculative Philosophers,* ed. Commins and Linscott, pp. 92 ff. Random House, New York, 1947. Quotations used by permission of the publisher.

[28] *Op. cit.,* pp. 110, 111.

[29] *Op. cit.,* pp. 150, 151.

CHAPTER III. THE "RELIGIOUS" VIEW IN EARLY AND MEDIEVAL CHRISTIAN THOUGHT

[1] See Chs. VIII and IX, below.

[2] C. Bigg, *The Christian Platonists of Alexandria,* Oxford University Press, Oxford, 1913.

[3] *On the Resurrection,* II.

[4] *Op. cit.,* VII.

[5] *Op. cit.,* VIII. Italics mine.

[6] *Against Heresies,* V. 33.i. Cf. 33–36. See Appendix to this chapter.

[7] The notion of man as a psychophysical unity, rather than a composite of two natures, is not only "modern" but also Biblical. See Chs. VIII and IX, below.

[8] *On the Soul, passim.*

[9] *On the Making of Man,* XII. 1–3.

[10] *Op. cit.,* XV. 3.

[11] *Loc. cit.*

[12] *On the Resurrection,* VIII.

¹³ *Miscellanies*, iii.

¹⁴ *On the Evidences of the Soul* and *Against Marcion*.

¹⁵ *On the Soul and the Resurrection, Ante-Nicene Fathers,* ed. Roberts and Donaldson, p. 442. Christian Literature Publishing Co., Buffalo, New York, 1886.

¹⁶ *Op. cit.,* pp. 455 ff.

¹⁷ *Confessions*, VII. 2.

¹⁸ *City of God*, XIII. 4.

¹⁹ For an examination of the meaning of " flesh " and " Spirit " in Saint Paul, which confirms this interpretation, see Ch. IX, below.

²⁰ *City of God*, XIV. 2, 3.

²¹ *Against Heresies*, I. 28. Tatian is also said to have been an extreme ascetic in practice.

²² Jerome, *Commentary on the Epistle to the Galatians*. Cf. Tertullian, *To His Wife,* I. 1, where marriage is described as " a voluptuous disgrace "; see also I.3, and his *Exhortation to Chastity,* ix. Cf. Saint Augustine, *Soliloquies,* I. 18, quoted below.

²³ *Miscellanies,* vi. 9. 71 and iii. 7. 59.

²⁴ *Op. cit.,* iii. 17. 103.

²⁵ *On the Soul and the Resurrection,* p. 448. Cf. p. 453. Italics mine.

²⁶ *Soliloquies,* 1. 18. Cf. Tatian and Tertullian, note 22, above.

²⁷ *Confessions,* VIII. 12.

²⁸ *On the Resurrection,* VIII.

²⁹ *Op. cit.,* X.

³⁰ *Dialogue with Trypho,* V.

³¹ E. G. Irenaeus, *Against Heresies,* V. 7. 1; Tertullian, *On the Soul, passim;* Gregory of Nyssa, *On the Soul and the Resurrection,* p. 437.

³² *On the Customs of the Church,* I. 27. 52, and *On the Gospel According to St. John,* 19.5.15.

³³ *On the Quantity of the Soul,* 13.21, and *On the Immortality of the Soul,* 17.

³⁴ *On the Resurrection,* X.

³⁵ *Against Heresies,* 5.31.2.

³⁶ *On the Soul and the Resurrection,* p. 443.

³⁷ *Op. cit.,* pp. 446, 447.

³⁸ *On the Predestination of the Saints,* XII. 24.

³⁹ Since the " end " presumably cannot be thought of as an event *in* time, it follows that to ask what the dead are doing " between " the time of their death and the " time " of the " last day " is a nonsense question.

[40] *Summa Theologiae,* Q. 75, Art. 5.
[41] *Op. cit.,* Q. 75, Art. 4. Cf. Art. 7.
[42] *Op. cit.,* Q. 75, Art. 7.
[43] *Op. cit.,* Q. 76, Art. 5. Cf. Q. 77, Art. 5.
[44] *Op. cit.,* Q. 90. Art. 4.
[45] *Op. cit.,* Q. 89, Art. 1. Cf. Q. 118, Art. 3.
[46] F. Coplestone, S. J., *A History of Philosophy,* Vol. II., p. 383. The Newman Press, Westminster, Maryland, 1950. Palm Publishers, Montreal, Canada. Quotations used by permission of the publishers.
[47] *Summa Theologiae,* Q. 93, Art. 4.
[48] *Op. cit.,* Q. 93, Art. 6. Contrast Justin Martyr, quoted on p. 53 above.
[49] *Op. cit.,* Q. 75, Art. 2.
[50] Cf. *op. cit.,* Q. 84, Art 2, and Q. 118, Art. 2.
[51] *Op. cit.,* Q. 75, Art. 6.
[52] *Op. cit.,* Q. 89, Art. 1.
[53] *Loc. cit.*
[54] Eugene R. Fairweather, "In Defense of Immortality," *Theology,* Vol. LVI, No. 396, June, 1953, p. 220.

CHAPTER IV. THE "RELIGIOUS" VIEW IN REFORMATION
AND MODERN THOUGHT

[1] "On the Liberty of a Christian Man," *Works,* Vol. II, p. 313. A. J. Holman Co., Philadelphia, Pennsylvania, 1915–1932.
[2] "The Magnificat," *Works,* Vol. III, p. 132.
[3] See Ch. IX, below.
[4] "The Magnificat," *loc. cit.*
[5] *Conversations with Luther,* trans. and ed. Smith and Gallinger, p. 122. The Pilgrim Press, Boston, Massachusetts, 1915.
[6] *Institutes,* II.XIV.1. Cf. I.XV.2.
[7] *Op. cit.* I.XV.7. Cf. I.XV.33. Cf. Saint Thomas Aquinas, quoted on p. 65 above and contrast Justin Martyr, quoted on p. 53 above.
[8] A. C. McGiffert, *See Protestant Thought Before Kant,* Ch. V. Duckworth & Co., London, 1919.
[9] *Table-Talk of Martin Luther,* trans. and ed. W. Hazlitt, DXIX. George Bell & Sons, London, 1902.
[10] *Conversations with Luther, loc. cit.*
[11] *See the Commentary on Peter and Jude,* trans. E. H. Gillet, New York, 1859, pp. 312 ff. Also *Works,* Vol. VI, pp. 287 ff., and *Works,*

Vol. XIV, sections 35–39. Lenker Edition, Luther Press, Minneapolis, Minnesota, 1903–1910.

[12] *Works,* Lenker Edition, Vol. XIII, p. 29.

[13] " The Magnificat," p. 132.

[14] *Institutes,* III.XXV.6.

[15] *Loc. cit.*

[16] J. V. L. Casserley, *The Retreat from Christianity,* p. 24.

[17] *The Renaissance Philosophy of Man,* ed. Cassirer, *et al.,* pp. 205, 206. University of Chicago Press, Chicago, 1948. Quotations reprinted by permission of the publisher.

[18] *Op. cit.,* pp. 224, 225. Italics mine.

[19] *Op. cit.,* pp. 272 and 279.

[20] *Discourse on Method,* V.

[21] *Op. cit.,* IV.

[22] *Op. cit.,* V. Cf. *Meditations,* **VI.**

[23] *Loc. cit.*

[24] *Op. cit.,* IV. Italics mine.

[25] *Op. cit.,* V.

[26] *Loc. cit.*

[27] G. Ryle, *The Concept of Mind,* Hutchinson's University Library, London, 1950.

[28] Both Luther and Calvin explicitly denied the doctrine of free will, in anything like the Renaissance sense: See Luther, *The Bondage of the Will,* pp. 76–79. Wm. B. Eerdmans Publishing Co., Grand Rapids, Michigan, 1931; and Calvin, *Institutes,* II, II, 8, and II, II, 27.

[29] W. McDougall, *Body and Mind,* p. 55. Methuen & Co., London, 1911. A quotation from a Letter to Arnauld, dated March 29, 1690.

[30] *Op. cit.,* p. 56; quoted from the *Monadologie,* par. 79.

[31] *Treatise of Human Nature,* I.IV.6.

[32] See Ch. VII, below.

[33] *Loc. cit.*

CHAPTER V. THE SCIENTIFIC EVIDENCE

[1] See Chs. VIII and IX, below.

[2] For the physiological information that follows I am indebted to W. McDougall, *Body and Mind,* pp. 102 ff., and Sir Charles Sherrington, *Man on His Nature, passim.* Doubleday & Co., New York, 1953.

[3] I have borrowed here from K. G. Collier, *The Science of Humanity,* pp. 58 ff. Nelson, London, 1950 and V. H. Mottram, *The Physical Basis of Personality,* Ch. VIII. Penguin Books, London, 1952. The four books mentioned in notes 2 and 3 are all concerned with the body-soul problem, chiefly from the scientific point of view but with sympathy for the " religious " view.

[4] *The Science of Humanity,* p. 49.

[5] Cf. *The Science of Humanity,* pp. 17 ff., and *The Physical Basis of Personality,* Chs. I to VI.

[6] R. Benedict, *Patterns of Culture,* p. 2. Mentor Books, New York, 1946.

[7] *Op. cit.,* p. 15.

[8] Benedict's phrase.

[9] F. Engels, *Socialism, Utopian and Scientific,* p. 51. International Publishers, New York, 1935.

[10] *Capital, The Communist Manifesto, and Other Writings,* ed. Max Eastman, p. 8. The Modern Library, New York, 1932.

[11] *Op. cit.,* p. 318.

[12] " Theses on Feuerbach," appended to F. Engels, *Ludwig Feuerbach,* p. 77. Foreign Languages Publishing House, Moscow, 1946.

[13] See pp. 96 ff. below.

[14] See Ch. X, below.

[15] S. Freud, *An Outline of Psycho-Analysis,* p. 1. Hogarth Press, London, 1949.

[16] *Op. cit.,* p. 2.

[17] S. Freud, *The Ego and the Id,* p. 82. Hogarth Press, London, 1927.

[18] *Op. cit.,* p. 39.

[19] S. Freud, *A General Introduction to Psycho-Analysis,* p. 310. The Garden City Publishing Co., Inc., New York, 1938.

[20] See Part III, below.

CHAPTER VI. SCIENTIFIC NATURALISM

[1] In many respects this chapter is a summary of my earlier work, *Scientism, Man, and Religion,* although some new considerations and arguments are included here.

[2] C. D. Broad, *Mind and Its Place in Nature,* pp. 622, 623; cf. p. 614. Kegan Paul, London, 1925.

[3] K. Marx, *Capital,* Vol. I., p. xxx. trans. Moore and Aveling. Allen & Unwin Ltd., London, 1938.

[4] N. Lenin, *Materialism and Empirio-Criticism*, p. 34. Foreign Languages Publishing House, Moscow, 1943.

[5] *Op. cit.*, p. 40.

[6] *Op. cit.*, pp. 249–251.

[7] *Op. cit.*, p. 40.

[8] *Op. cit.*, p. 44.

[9] *Op. cit.*, p. 38.

[10] *Ludwig Feuerbach*, p. 30.

[11] *Materialism and Empirio-Criticism*, p. 38.

[12] *Loc. cit.*

[13] Quoted by Engels in *Socialism, Utopian and Scientific*, p. 11.

[14] *Ludwig Feuerbach, loc. cit.*

[15] *An Outline of Psycho-Analysis*, p. 65; cf. p. 1.

[16] *Loc. cit.*

[17] *Op. cit.*, p. 2.

[18] *Loc. cit.*

[19] *The Ego and the Id*, p. 31.

[20] *An Outline of Psycho-Analysis*, p. 1.

[21] *The Ego and the Id*, pp. 82, 83.

[22] " Theses on Feuerbach " in *Ludwig Feuerbach*, p. 77.

[23] *The Basic Writings of Sigmund Freud*, ed. A. A. Brill, p. 161. Modern Library, Inc., New York, 1938.

[24] *The Ego and the Id*, p. 82.

[25] G. Ryle, *The Concept of Mind*.

[26] *Ludwig Feuerbach*, p. 30.

[27] W. Temple, *Nature, Mind and God*, Chs. V and VIII. Cf. Lenin, *Materialism and Empirio-Criticism*, p. 38.

[28] *Patterns of Culture*, pp. 122, 123.

[29] Cf. C. S. Lewis, *The Abolition of Man*, pp. 41 ff. Oxford University Press, London, 1944.

[30] Brock Chisholm, " The Psychiatry of Enduring Peace and Social Progress," *Psychiatry*, Vol. 9, No. I, p. 9.

[31] *Op. cit.*, p. 10.

[32] *Patterns of Culture*, pp. 228–231.

CHAPTER VII. THE MEANING OF " SPIRIT "

[1] *Materialism and Empirio-Criticism*, p. 40.

[2] *Op. cit.*, p. 38.

[3] *Loc. cit.*

[4] Cf. Sherrington, *op. cit.*, Ch. III, and pp. 146 and 177.

[5] Cf. Sherrington, *op. cit.,* p. 87.

[6] *Patterns of Culture,* pp. 42, 43.

[7] F. Engels, *Anti-Duhring,* p. 125. International Publishers, New York, 1939. This definition of freedom was not invented by the Marxists. It is found in Stoicism, in Spinoza, and in some types of Christian theology (in a somewhat different form; cf. the Second Collect for Morning Prayer in *The Book of Common Prayer:* " Whose service is perfect freedom ").

[8] *The Ego and the Id,* p. 72, footnote.

[9] David Roberts, *Psycho-Therapy and a Christian View of Man,* p. 110. Scribners, New York, 1950.

[10] *Socialism, Utopian and Scientific,* pp. 72, 73. The German word, here translated " ascent," is *Ursprung;* it might better be translated " leap," which would make the statement even stronger.

[11] See Ch. X, below.

[12] I referred briefly to the distinction between subject and object at the end of *Scientism, Man, and Religion* (pp. 175 ff.). What follows here is an elaboration of the somewhat cryptic remarks made there.

[13] *An Outline of Psycho-Analysis,* p. 65.

[14] *The Positive Philosophy of August Comte,* trans. Martineau, p. 7. D. Appleton & Co., London, 1853.

[15] A. J. Toynbee, *A Study of History,* p. 60. Abridgment by D. C. Somervell, Oxford University Press, London, 1946.

[16] See Appendix to this chapter.

[17] *The Concept of Mind, passim.*

[18] It is only fair to say that Ryle in one passage, though perhaps only one, indicates clearly that in his view man transcends the rest of nature, in the sense of differing from it in certain fundamental respects. He writes (*op. cit.,* p. 328): " Man need not be degraded to a machine by being denied to be a ghost in a machine. He might, after all, be a sort of animal, namely, a higher mammal. There has yet to be ventured the hazardous leap to the hypothesis that perhaps he is a man."

[19] *Phaedo,* 98o9.

CHAPTER VIII. THE BIBLICAL ATTITUDE TO THE PHYSICAL

[1] See Ch. I.

[2] See Ch. II.

[3] See Ch. VII.

[4] See Ch. X, below.

[5] For example, Clement of Alexandria, *Miscellanies,* iii. 17. 103.

[6] It is extremely interesting that the terms translated here as "natural" and "spiritual" are, in the Greek, not *sōmatikon* and *psychikon,* which a dualist would certainly have used, but rather *psychikon* and *pneumatikon.* See Ch. X, below.

[7] Ch. IX, below.

[8] J. A. T. Robinson, *The Body,* pp. 76, 77. Student Christian Movement Press, London, 1952. Alec R. Allenson, Inc., Chicago. Quotations used by permission of S.C.M. Press and Alec R. Allenson, Inc.

[9] Cf. *The Body,* p. 78, footnote: " The scene of the Messianic Kingdom, and therefore of the body of glory, is a renovated earth "; see also pp. 92, 93. Cf. *The Resurrection of Christ,* A. M. Ramsey, The Westminster Press, London, 1946, pp. 115, 116: " Yet this divine Kingdom will not be removed from nature and history; for in it both nature and history will be ' clothed upon ' and fulfilled . . . Nature will not be discarded, in order that man's soul alone may be salvaged and saved. The life of nature here and the life of the body which links us to nature will not be as a ladder, whereon we may climb to heaven and fling it aside when the ascent is finished. Rather will all that God has made have its place and counterpart in the new heaven and the new earth. ' Immortality ' will be put on; but ' this mortal ' will find there its clothing and its home."

[10] *Nature, Man and God,* p. 478. Italics mine.

[11] H. Wheeler Robinson, *The Religious Ideas of the Old Testament,* Ch. IV. Duckworth, London, 1913. See also his essay on " Hebrew Psychology " in *The People and the Book,* ed. A. S. Peake. Oxford University Press, 1925.

[12] " Hebrew Psychology," p. 362. Italics mine.

[13] *Op. cit.,* p. 355.

[14] *Op. cit.,* p. 366.

[15] *The Religious Ideas of the Old Testament,* p. 83.

[16] " Hebrew Psychology," pp. 362 ff.

[17] *Op. cit.,* p. 382.

[18] *Op. cit.,* p. 366.

[19] *The Religious Ideas of the Old Testament,* p. 92.

[20] *Op. cit.,* p. 97.

[21] *Op. cit.,* p. 83.

[22] " Hebrew Psychology," p. 366.

[23] *The Religious Ideas of the Old Testament,* pp. 87–94.

[24] *The Religious Ideas of the Old Testament,* p. 97.

CHAPTER IX. " BODY " AND " SOUL " IN THE NEW TESTAMENT

[1] E. R. Fairweather, " In Defense of Immortality," *Theology,* Vol. LVI, No. 396, pp. 219, 220.

[2] Cf. the version of this saying in Luke 12:4, 5 which seems to support our interpretation.

[3] My colleague Dr. F. W. Beare, who is a leading New Testament scholar, strongly disputes my exegesis of John 11:26. He points out that the construction here — " shall not die [or, as I put it, " be dead "] *eis ton aiōna* " — has an exact parallel in John 13:8: " Shall not wash my feet *eis ton aiōna."* The latter must be translated, " Shall *never* wash my feet." Therefore, he argues, the former must be translated, " Shall never die." I admit the force of this argument, of course. Nevertheless, it seems to me quite possible that the Greek word *aiōn,* where it is connected with the question of *death,* has its technical meaning, viz., " the age to come," while elsewhere it is combined with the negative in the ordinary way to mean " never." I attach a good deal of importance to the fact that phrases of this kind in Saint John are usually followed immediately by some such clause as, " And I will raise him up at the last day." Dr. Beare can only explain this by saying that the author of the Fourth Gospel is simply combining two different ideas, namely, the resurrection of the body that was part of the new gospel he had received, and the immortality of the soul that was part of his earlier philosophy, and that he did not perceive that the two ideas were incompatible. This may be the proper explanation. If so, we should simply have to recognize that the " religious " doctrine of the immortality of the soul has crept in here, but is quite out of keeping with the main New Testament teaching. I myself, however, have more respect for the intellectual acumen of the author of this Gospel, and therefore prefer the exegesis I have given in the text. After all, the same linguistic construction may be used in different contexts with different meanings.

[4] *The Body,* p. 11. In what follows I am heavily indebted to this work, which was cited in the notes to Ch. VIII.

[5] *Israel* 1–11, J. Pedersen, p. 171. Quoted in *The Body,* p. 14.

[6] *The Body, loc. cit.*

[7] " Hebrew Psychology," p. 366.

[8] See e.g., Professor White's essay cited in Ch. II, above.

[9] *The Body,* pp. 17–19.

[10] See Eph. 5:28; II Cor. 7:5; Col. 1:24; II Cor. 4:11.

[11] *The Body,* p. 19. Cf. Job 10:4; Isa. 31:3

[12] *Op. cit.,* pp. 25, 26. His references are to Rom. 16:18; Phil. 3:19; I Cor. 7:32; Gal. 5:16, 24; Rom. 13:14; Eph. 2:3; Col. 2:23; 3:2.

[13] *Op. cit.,* p. 28.

[14] *Op. cit.,* p. 13, footnote.

[15] *Op. cit.,* p. 26.

[16] Cf. Rom. 8:10; 7:22–25; Col. 3:5.

[17] *The Body,* pp. 30, 31.

[18] *Op. cit.,* p. 31.

[19] *Loc. cit.*

[20] *Op. cit.,* pp. 31, 32, footnote.

[21] *Op. cit.,* p. 31.

[22] *Op. cit.,* p. 82.

[23] See Appendix to this chapter.

CHAPTER X. THE NATURE AND DESTINY OF MAN

[1] Ch. VII, above.

[2] *Nature, Man and God,* p. 366.

[3] Again this is said from the theological and not from the critical point of view.

[4] C. Ryder Smith, *The Biblical Doctrine of Man,* p. 182. Epworth Press, London, 1951.

[5] As, for instance, by Engels in the long passage quoted in Ch. VII, above.

[6] N. Berdyaev, *Slavery and Freedom,* p. 132. Charles Scribner's Sons, New York, 1944.

[7] *Summa Contra Gentiles,* IV. 2.2.

[8] *See* E. Fromm, *Escape from Freedom,* pp. 141 ff. Rhinehart & Co., Inc., New York, 1941; and *Man for Himself,* pp. 8 ff., 142 ff. Rhinehart & Co., Inc., New York, 1947.

[9] The Second Collect for Morning Prayer.

[10] *Nature, Man and God,* p. 397.

[11] Cf. the Collect for the Fourth Sunday after Easter in *The Book of Common Prayer:* " O Almighty God, who alone canst order the unruly wills and affections of sinful men; Grant unto thy people, that they may *love the thing which thou commandest,* and *desire that which thou dost promise;* that so, among the sundry and manifold changes of the world, our hearts may surely there be fixed, where true joys are to be found." Also the Collect for the

Fourteenth Sunday after Trinity, with its similar phrases: "that we may obtain that which thou dost promise, make us *to love that which thou dost command.*" These collects reflect a genuine Christian ethics.

[12] David Cairns, *The Image of God in Man,* pp. 29 ff. and Ch. XIV. Student Christian Movement Press, London, 1953.

[13] Cf. Luke 10:9–11, and II Cor. 6:2.

[14] Usually translated "within you," but the Greek word could mean "among," and the eschatological context of the saying suggest that something like the latter is correct.

[15] R. Niebuhr, *The Nature and Destiny of Man,* p. 1. Charles Scribner's Sons, New York, 1941.

INDEX